AVID

READER

PRESS

ALSO BY BRIAN MORTON

The Dylanist

Starting Out in the Evening

A Window Across the River

Breakable You

Florence Gordon

Tasha

A Son's Memoir

Brian Morton

Avid Reader Press

New York   London   Toronto   Sydney   New Delhi

AVID READER PRESS
An Imprint of Simon & Schuster, Inc.
1230 Avenue of the Americas
New York, NY 10020

First Avid Reader Press hardcover edition April 2022

AVID READER PRESS and colophon are
trademarks of Simon & Schuster, Inc.

For information about special discounts for bulk purchases,
please contact Simon & Schuster Special Sales
at 1-866-506-1949 or business@simonandschuster.com.

The Simon & Schuster Speakers Bureau can bring authors to your live event.
For more information or to book an event contact the
Simon & Schuster Speakers Bureau at 1-866-248-3049
or visit our website at www.simonspeakers.com.

Interior design by Ruth Lee-Mui

Manufactured in the United States of America

1   3   5   7   9   10   8   6   4   2

Library of Congress Cataloging-in-Publication Data has been applied for.

ISBN 978-1-9821-7893-2
ISBN 978-1-9821-7895-6 (ebook)

For Heather

On March 13, 2010, driving at night in a thunderstorm, my mother got stuck on a flooded road near the Hackensack River. Her car stalled out and the electrical system failed, so pressing on the horn yielded no sound. She didn't have her cell phone with her. The river forced its way inside the car, covering her ankles, moving up to her knees. She was eighty-five years old and in poor health and she knew that if she left the car she'd be dragged down into the water. She was sure she was going to die.

I was living with my family in Westchester. The rain had been crazy all day. In the morning I'd promised my kids that we'd go out to the toy store and the library, but although we wouldn't have to travel more than half a mile, the storm was so wild that I wasn't sure about leaving the house at all. Heather was at a conference that weekend, and I had the kids on my own. Finally I told myself it couldn't be so terrible to drive a few blocks, and I took them to the toy store. Driving there turned out to be an exercise in not letting them see how frightened I was—I could barely make out the road—and after they'd each picked a toy, I decided to skip the library and take them back home.

My niece, who was in high school, was giving a dance recital that night, but the drive took an hour in good conditions and would have been a nightmare during a storm like this. I wrote to my sister, Melinda, with apologies; she told me it was fine, and added that our mother was still planning to attend.

I can't say I was surprised. My mother was like a child in many ways. She'd never been good at knowing her own limitations or thinking ahead. One of my early memories was of an evening when she took Melinda and me to see our grandparents off at Penn Station after they'd visited us in New Jersey. I was four and my sister was seven. Our grandparents were taking a train back to Pittsburgh. She felt it important to help them find their seats, though they were only in their early sixties and were perfectly capable of doing this themselves, and she felt it important to stay with them, soaking up every minute of togetherness, even after the announcement that anyone without a ticket had to leave the train. She told my sister and me to get off and wait for her on the platform. I don't know what made her want to postpone leaving until the last possible moment. I don't think there was any real reason; I think it was just hard for her to leave. That was one of the first things you got to know about my mother, if you knew her at all. It was hard for her to let anybody go.

My sister and I waited outside the train. We heard a second announcement, and then a third, and then we saw the train start to move.

I don't remember what I was thinking. I don't remember if my sister said anything. But I do remember that the train began moving and my mother wasn't with us and I didn't know what we were going to do.

Finally she emerged in the space between two cars. She looked at us, smiled nervously, looked down at the swiftly moving plat-form, and jumped.

My mother, it should be mentioned here, was not a graceful woman. She'd never been athletic, and a providential moment of nimbleness was not bestowed upon her now. She leapt from the train in an odd way—the position of her body reminded me of an angel in a cartoon, reclining on a cloud while playing a harp—and landed heavily on the platform, and cried out in pain.

At the distance of sixty years, I can see that she was lucky. The force of the fall was taken by the fleshiest part of her body. She didn't break any bones. She didn't hit her head. She didn't suffer any serious injuries. But for months she bore a frightening bruise, covering most of her thigh and part of her backside. (She showed it to us more than once, even though, for me at least, once was more than enough. She might have thought it was educational for us in some way.)

To my four-year-old mind, this adventure seemed to say two things about her. Her leap and her bruise seemed to mark her as both heroic and unbalanced. I can't deny that I thought there was something glorious about the sight of her leaping from the train, but neither can I deny that I understood, even then, that there was something off about it too, something that set her apart from other grown-ups, and not in a good way.

All of which is to say that in 2010, when I learned my mother was planning to attend the recital, it didn't even occur to me to try to talk her out of it. I thought it was foolish, but I also thought it was just her, and I'd learned long ago that when I tried to talk her out of doing something she was intent on, I had no chance.

I did whatever I did with the kids that night. I imagine I made them some nutritionally questionable dinner—chicken fingers for Emmett, mac and cheese for Gabe—and watched a movie with them and waited eagerly for them to fall asleep. After that I'm sure I either wrote or wasted time on the internet. The storm didn't die down. If you care to look it up, just search for "storm" and "March 13, 2010" and "New Jersey." I remember that I thought about my mother once or twice, wondering how she'd fared in the miserable weather. I wrote her an email at around midnight, and was surprised when I didn't hear back—she liked to stay up late, and she was always on her computer—but I have to admit I didn't think about it very much. I assumed things had turned out fine.

In the morning I checked my email and saw that she'd written to me at two. She told me what had happened—she'd finally been found by the police as they patrolled the flooded streets—and said that it had been the worst night of her life.

A few days later, Melinda visited her and noticed that her balance was off. She took her to her doctor, who sent them to Englewood Hospital to determine whether she'd had a stroke.

I met them at the hospital. My mother had already had a few tests and they were waiting for results. She was sitting in one of those backless gowns, which seem designed to humiliate you and thereby render you willing to do what you're told. She was normally an irrepressibly chatty person, but now she was sitting on the examining room table with a doleful expression, not saying a word. Occasionally she swung her legs in the air, looking like a disappointed child.

When she did speak, it was hard to tell if she was slurring her words. If you listen carefully to anyone at all and ask yourself whether they're slurring their words a little, it can be hard to be sure.

I was worrying about many things.

I was worrying about her, of course. I was worrying about how much damage she might have suffered; I was worried about whether she was going to be able to continue living on her own. But I was also worrying about myself. I had successfully kept her at arm's length for many years, not really doing much for her except having dinner with her from time to time, and this was comfortable for me. Now it seemed that I might have to call on different capacities in myself, and I didn't want to.

You find out who you are at funerals. You find out who you are, I mean, at the funerals of old friends, because the families of the one who died, their inhibitions loosened by their grief, will speak to you in an unguarded way, and sometimes they'll tell you things about yourself that they wouldn't have told you otherwise.

In the months before my mother's stroke, I'd attended the funerals of two old friends. When I went to Seth Kaplan's funeral and expressed my condolences to his sister, she, for some reason, launched into a long account of her memories of me from back in junior high school, which, it turned out, weren't memories of me at all. They were memories of my mother.

"All I can remember is these phone calls from your mother," she said. "It'd be dinnertime on a weekday night and your mother would call, hysterical. 'Is Brian there? I can't find Brian. I've been calling everywhere. I've called the hospitals, I've called the police.' And it would only be six o'clock. I didn't get it. 'Is Brian there?'"

At Robert Gordon's funeral, Robert's mother said much the same thing. "She was always calling. She was always frantic. I used to wonder how you could put up with it. *I* could barely put up with it."

When you're young, it's hard to see your parents in context. Your parents *are* the context. Your parents are the people who've mapped the world for you, and it can take years to discover that their maps are imperfect or incomplete. You think they're teaching you about how a person should be; it takes a long time to understand that they're merely teaching you about how they want you to be.

It took me years, even decades, to fashion a relationship with my mother in which I could affirm my love for her while placing limits on her. And now, in the hospital room, as she sat on the examining table and swung her legs childishly, at the same time as I was worried for her, I was thinking with dread that I was probably going to have to let her much more consistently into my life.

She said she wanted a soda, so I walked down the hall to a bank of vending machines. When I started back toward the room, my mother wasn't in my line of sight. I could only see my sister. She was looking out the window in a meditative silence.

When we were young, my sister had been my leader, my ideal co-conspirator, my guide. In recent years she'd endured a lacerating illness and a grueling treatment regimen. She was working six days a week at a demanding job. I knew she'd be willing to do most of the work of caring for our mother; I knew it would be wrong to let her.

I gave my mother the soda.

"Where do you want to have dinner?" she said. "You're staying around for dinner, right?"

How can you see your parents clearly? How can you see them as they are?

Sometimes you'll notice a middle-aged son or daughter reacting to a very old parent with an outsized irritability—rolling their eyeballs and sighing at whatever the parent says. It's as if the parent's mere presence has sent the child tumbling through time, all the way back to middle school. How can you make sure you're not that son or daughter?

I'm wondering about these questions because I've written about my mother before, and I don't think I even came close to getting it right.

Decades ago, after my father died, I wrote a novel that began simply as an attempt to put my memories of him on paper. My mother was in the novel too, of course. But I don't think I treated her fairly.

The portrait of my father was bathed in the glow of idealization. It's easier to idealize the parent who's dead. It's easier, also, to idealize the parent who was ever-distant than the parent who never knew when to leave.

And it's easier to satirize your voluble Jewish mother than your moody Irish father. This is one of the basic laws of fiction.

I didn't show it to her when I was working on it, because I knew that what I wrote about her would hurt her, and I didn't see the point of going out of my way to hurt her by showing her a novel that might end up in a drawer. (This was back in the days of typewriters, when unpublished novels really did end up in drawers.)

When it was finally accepted for publication, I gave her a copy. I handed the box of xeroxed pages to her after she came into the city to meet me for dinner one night. I can't remember if I said anything to try to prepare her.

The next morning, I got a message on my answering machine.

"Brian? This is your former mother . . ."

There were some things she said I absolutely had to take out— "I won't be able to face people in Teaneck, the way you wrote about me"—and I did what she asked. But taking out the more egregious details didn't help much, since she found the portrait as a whole so wounding.

After the novel, which was called *The Dylanist*, was published, I told a couple of friends that I felt guilty about having hurt her, and both of them said that it's in the portrait of the mother that the novel's warmth and life reside. The father is like a mythical figure; the mother is real.

But I don't think she ever came to see it that way. I know she looked at the novel often during the thirty years in which she outlived him, because rereading the parts about my father made her feel closer to him, but it must have been painful to go back to the book for that sense of connection and to keep coming across descriptions of herself that she found embarrassing. I don't think it occurred to me that I had much of a choice. Her eccentricities made it hard for me to resist a comic portrayal.

She was a woman—to take an example more or less at random—who found it impossible to imagine a situation that wouldn't be enhanced by her presence.

When my sister, having a hard time in high school, said she thought she might benefit from talking to a therapist, my mother said, "I can be your therapist. Talk to me."

"I think I'd like to talk to a professional," Melinda said.

"I know more about psychology than most psychologists," my mother said. In college she'd taken a psychology class.

One summer when I was in my twenties, I went to France, and when I was there I met someone—a subtle young woman named Sabine, who was getting a doctorate in philosophy. Sabine made plans to visit me in New York that fall. I mentioned this to my sister, and when my mother got wind of it, she offered to drive me to JFK to pick her up.

"It'll be cheaper than a cab," she pointed out. "Cheaper than the subway."

"That's an interesting idea," I said. "'Thank you for traveling five thousand miles to stay with me. Say hi to my mom.'"

"You won't have to tell her I'm your mother. She won't even know we're related. I can just be the driver."

I tried to picture this—my mother, perhaps wearing a chauffeur's cap, pretending not to know me.

Great screen romances as reimagined by Tasha Morton. *Casablanca*: Bogart telling Bergman they'll always have Paris, as they remember the magical evenings they spent there with his mom.

Titanic, with Leonardo DiCaprio's mother bobbing up and down in the water next to him.

The remarkable thing about her offer was that she was serious. She didn't seem to see that it might not be a treat to have her there.

It wasn't remarkable at all, really. It was Tasha.

But she was also a woman who, after the death of her husband—my father—had fallen into a state of despondency that she never really made her way out of. Who couldn't bring herself to discard or give away his clothing or his cuff links or even his cigarettes, though his smoking had driven her to despair. Who, speaking at her old friend Ruby's funeral a year after my father's death, said three or four sentences about Ruby, and then, without realizing she was wandering off in the wrong direction, spent the rest of her time at the podium talking about him.

Write about her tragically or write about her comically: I didn't want to write about her tragically, and when I was working on my first novel, I don't think I could see any possibilities but those.

What I didn't pause to think about was that she was much more than the sum of her eccentricities. No man is a hero to his valet, the saying goes, and few mothers are heroes to their sons.

What I didn't pause to consider were things like these:

She left home when she was sixteen. Somehow she had the strength to do that, in 1941. Her first act after leaving home was an act of self-creation: she chose her name. Her given name was Esther, but in the Bronx of the 1940s, Esther was the name of every third girl on the street. She named herself Tasha, partly because she

11

liked the sound and partly because it wasn't the name of anyone she knew.

She was already working—she was the first-ever copy girl at the *Daily Worker*, a fact that she often cited proudly. Later she got a job at a labor union, the United Office and Professional Workers of America, where she met my father, who was an organizer there. When he dragged his feet about getting married, she took herself off to the newly founded state of Israel ("I told him to shit or get off the pot," as she often put it) and lived on a kibbutz for six months. In the early 1950s, when she was in her late twenties, she began studying at NYU. She left school to have my sister and me, and resumed her education ten years later, receiving her BA and then her master's in education, and started teaching in the public schools when she was almost forty. In the late 1960s and 1970s, when the alternative education movement was flourishing, she led an "open classroom" arrangement in a public school. She and two other teachers formed a team for kindergarten and first-grade students. There was a reading room, an arithmetic room, and a science room, and the kids would spend time in whatever rooms they wanted. Her theory was that by the end of the year, each child would want to learn everything, and every year, her theory was proved correct. This was the era in which becoming a public school teacher, in the eyes of many people, was an idealistic and exciting choice, a calling, and in which, in some parts of the country, experimentation in the classroom was encouraged. Our house was filled with the classics of that moment: *Teaching as a Subversive Activity, How Children Fail* and *How Children Learn, Summerhill, Crisis in the Classroom, Growing Up Absurd.*

Her classroom was a place of playfulness and warmth. It was also the most memorable educational environment I've ever been in. When you visited, you'd never find her at the head of the room and the children in docile rows. Instead, the children would be sitting at little tables or on the carpet, working intently by themselves or in groups, while she circulated among them, helping one kid with his arithmetic, helping a group of kids with something they were reading, stopping with another group just to joke around. Sometimes you'd find her on the carpet, a few of her students around her, all of them doing puzzles or math games or sounding out words together.

By the end of the 1970s, the national mood had changed, and "student-centered learning" had lost the support of superintendents and school boards. Experiments like my mother's team-teaching model weren't supported anymore, but she continued to teach along open-classroom principles until she retired. She believed that children have a natural love of learning and that they should be the subjects rather than the objects of education. You could say that she was dedicated to helping her students become independent-minded people.

It occurs to me only as I write this that my father's ideas about union organizing were the same as my mother's ideas about teaching. Organizers were people who served others. Their job was to help workers clarify their needs and develop their skills. The organizer was never the star of the show; the organizer—in language he never would have used—was really something closer to a midwife.

Starting in 1964, the year we moved to Teaneck, she went to

board of education meetings every week. After she retired from teaching in 1985, she successfully ran for a seat on the board, and she kept being reelected until 2005, when she was eighty. (For years she'd had the support of the hundreds of parents whose children she'd taught, but finally most of them had either died or moved to Florida.)

But this is the thing I found remarkable: after she finally lost her seat on the board, she didn't walk away—she continued to attend the meetings every week, no longer as a teacher or a board member, but as a citizen. I loved it that she cared that much about education and the town where she lived.

Caring about education, caring about the town, entailed fighting for a vision of what they might be. After we moved to Teaneck, she and my father joined an interracial organization, the North East Community Organization, that was fighting the racist redlining practices still legal at the time, whereby real estate salesmen would steer white families to one section of town, black families to another, and later that year we moved to the section of town that white people were told to stay away from.

(My parents were proud but absentminded homeowners. I was supposed to mow the lawn every weekend, but I was always too busy watching TV, and as the lawn got shaggier and shaggier, my parents either didn't notice or didn't care. One day our next-door neighbor told them, "You're unusual white folks. You move into the neighborhood and bring the property values down." They made me mow the lawn after that.)

I'm not embellishing her history here, by the way. Not making her more of an activist than she was. You can look it up. Google "Tasha Morton" and "NECO."

When I write down all these details, what I see is a life that was successful, by any measure of success that has meaning to me. What I see is a life that was devoted to making a contribution. What I see is the life of a woman who gave of herself as fully as she could. And I'm not sure I got any of that onto the page.

So now I find myself wanting to return to her—to try to see her whole, as I didn't succeed in doing when she was alive.

It took the doctors several days of testing, but finally they determined that, as her internist had thought, she'd had a stroke.

Anticipating this, Heather and I had been visiting rehabilitation centers in the area. The Helen Hayes Hospital, in Rockland County, New York, was by far the best place we saw: it was clean and quiet, and the people who worked there seemed to know what they were doing. When Heather and I talked to her about it, I think she was touched that we'd taken the time to investigate.

She hadn't had a major stroke, which was a relief. Her balance was off and her speech was a little slurred and her memory was shaky—I heard her on the phone with friends, and in trying to explain what was going on with her, she kept forgetting the word "stroke"—but she didn't have any pronounced weakness on either side of her body or her face.

When we took her to Helen Hayes, I was filled with hope. My mother seemed grateful for our attention and eager to get better.

For years she'd been having health problems and refusing to do anything about them. Her hearing had been failing, but she didn't believe in hearing aids. She'd become somewhat incontinent but wouldn't see a urologist—"I don't need anybody looking around down there." Her driving had become so erratic that I wouldn't allow my children to be in a car with her; even driving on local streets that she'd been driving on for fifty years, she was like a fascinated tourist, taking her eyes off the road to appreciate the architectural features of the houses she passed, or like a nature enthusiast, delightedly turning her head to watch dogs or squirrels at play.

Now, I thought, she'll take her health and safety more seriously. Everything that can be fixed, we'll help her fix.

On the ride up to Rockland County she kept thanking us. She talked about how she was going to do everything they asked her to do so she could get well again.

I was imagining that as part of the great change, she would finally let us hire a cleaning person and maybe even consent to move out of her house.

Her house was operatically disordered. She never threw anything out and she never cleaned up after herself. She would read the newspaper or the mail and then just drop the papers wherever she happened to be sitting, and then she'd slip on them at three in the morning on her way to the bathroom. Twice she'd broken bones this way.

Once and only once, she'd allowed us to hire someone to come in and clean. The woman had filled fifteen trash bags with garbage and put them at the curb, and that night my mother had dragged them back to the kitchen and taken everything back out.

But now, it seemed, the stroke had sobered her up. "I understand I have to change," she kept saying. Now she would listen to reason. She'd let us hire a cleaning person, who would visit every week; she'd let us hire landscapers, and, in contrast to the two occasions when we'd done this in the past, this time she wouldn't threaten to sue them. Or, even better than any of that, she'd let us find her a nice apartment in an assisted living facility. It seemed obvious that she'd enjoy her life more if she lived in a place where her everyday needs were taken care of. On the ride to Rockland County, I talked to her about this, painting a picture of how appealing life could be if she had a clean apartment, a place that wasn't mildewed, a place where you could find a spot to sit down. Heather and I could visit her with the kids and spend evenings with her, playing Monopoly or watching TV. We wouldn't have to confine our New Jersey visits to restaurants.

I was excited. The small stroke could be a turning point.

"They keep asking me such silly questions," she said on her second day there.

"Like what?"

"Today that skinny guy asked me something like, 'If you have a five-pound turkey and you have to cook it forty-five minutes for each pound . . .' How should I know? I haven't cooked in years!"

"I don't think they were really concerned with cooking a turkey," I said. "I think they were trying to see if you could do the math."

She considered that for a moment and then shrugged.

"So what if I can't do the math anymore?" she said. "What do I need it for?"

I admired her cheerfulness. She wasn't mourning what had befallen her. She seemed to think the capacities she'd been left with were all she needed.

But I was worried about her lack of understanding. The skinny guy—an occupational therapist—was trying to assess her cognitive state in order to understand how best to treat her, and she didn't seem to get that at all.

Before the week was out, it was clear that she wasn't going to get better at Helen Hayes. She complained about the medical staff; she complained about the aides; she complained about the TV in her room, which didn't have MSNBC and therefore came between her and her beloved Rachel Maddow. Patients were expected to eat

at a communal table, and although the dining room was beautiful, big and bright and clean, with a view of the long sweep of the
Hudson River, she didn't want to eat with people she didn't know
and insisted on taking her meals in her room.

She was given an appointment with the resident audiologist,
but she refused to see him.

"Mom—" I said when she told me about it.

"Mom what?"

"You could use a pair of hearing aids."

"Sylvia Lowenstein at the Jewish Center got a hearing aid. I
think she paid five thousand dollars. And do you think she hears
any better with those things? Whenever you talk to her, you still
have to shout."

"So if Sylvia Lowenstein's hearing aids don't do any good,
hearing aids are therefore useless?"

"That's right."

"That doesn't make logical sense, Mom."

"Logical sense? I know more about logic than most logicians.
I'm a great logician."

She settled back contentedly on her pillows.

Those were her thoughts about the audiologist. Her thoughts
about the psychologist were not dissimilar.

"She's nothing but a nudnik. She won't stop asking me all
these questions."

"That's what a therapist is supposed to do, Mom."

"Why is she interested in all that foolishness? None of it
matters."

"That's not true. All of it matters."

"How does it matter how I feel about anything? I had a whatchamacallit—"

"A stroke?"

"I had one of those and I need to get better. Some nudnik asking silly questions isn't going to help. How is that going to help?"

"You want to know how that could help? You really want to know?"

"Yes. I do. Tell me. I'm all ears."

"I'll tell you how it could help. You keep saying that you can't even think about whether to sell the house until you clean the house. But you haven't been able to clean the house. You've been talking about this for twenty years. If you talked to somebody, they might just be able to help you get to a point where you could clean the house up."

"How can she help me with that? Is she going to come over with a special broom?"

"She could help you get your thoughts clear."

"How is she going do that?"

"I don't know! If I knew that, I'd *be* a psychologist."

"She'll help me with that by getting me to talk about my childhood?"

"I just said I don't know!"

"That doesn't even make any sense. Anyway, I'm already making progress."

"You're making progress?"

21

"Yes. I'm starting to clean the place up."

"You are?"

"You should see the place."

"I was there the other day to get you your slippers. There are dead mice in the living room."

"That's an exaggeration. There aren't dead mice. Maybe there was one."

"There were two. They died in each other's arms."

"That's not a bad way to go," she said. "A lot of other mice would consider them lucky."

She had refused the audiologist, the urologist, and the shrink, and although she kept going to physical therapy, she wouldn't take it seriously.

"Now show me how we've learned to hold on to the banister," the therapist said, after patiently modeling it for her. They were in a room with a five-step stairway, a stairway to nowhere, designed especially for rehab patients.

My mother sent her hand diving toward the banister and then lifted it, pretending it was a plane driven by a stunt pilot.

"Watch out!" she said, sending it down again. "Crop duster! I'm crashing into Cary Grant!"

"I don't get that, but that's all right," the therapist said. "Now do it correctly for me."

My mother made her index finger and her middle finger walk up the banister. They did a little dance: two steps forward, one step back.

"It's Fred Astaire," she said.

"The sooner you take this seriously, the sooner you'll be able to go home," the therapist said.

"I'm taking it very seriously," my mother said. "Spaceship," she added, lifting her hand in a shuddering circular motion evidently meant to conjure up the idea of a flying saucer fighting its way out of the earth's gravitational field. I could sort of see it.

With the people who were there to help her, she either clowned around or she fought.

One evening when I was visiting, a nurse came in to check her blood pressure.

"What's that thing around your neck?" my mother said to her.

"Beg pardon?"

"What's that thing you're wearing?"

"This? It's a cross."

Here it comes, I thought.

"And who's the little guy in the diaper?"

The nurse smiled. "You know who it is. It's Jesus."

"You're a religious person?" my mother said.

"Yes. I'm Catholic."

"You're a nurse and you're a religious person."

The nurse seemed amused.

"Where's the contradiction?" she said.

"You're a nurse and you went to school to learn about the science of how to save people's lives, but you still believe in God. If God is all-powerful why doesn't *he* save everybody's life? What do we need you for?"

"God created the world, and then he stepped back to let us live in it," the nurse said.

"If God is all-powerful," my mother said—and I knew what was coming—"why did he let the Holocaust happen? Why did he kill my relatives?"

"He gave us our freedom," the nurse said again. "Whether we use it wisely or not is up to us."

"What about lynchings? Have you ever heard of Emmett Till? Would you call that using it wisely?"

"God doesn't step in," the nurse said, wrapping the blood pressure cuff around my mother's arm.

"But if he's all-powerful, and he sat there watching the Holocaust, and he sat there watching the slave trade, why do you think it's a good idea to worship him? You say he gave us our freedom to do what we want. Okay, so maybe he's not quite a mass murderer. He didn't do the Holocaust himself. But he stood by and watched it happen. What do you call someone who sees a mass murder and has the power to stop it and doesn't do anything? I don't know what I'd call him but I sure as hell wouldn't let him dangle around near my boobs to show everybody how much I love him."

I turned away, because I didn't want either of them to see me laughing.

"My son probably doesn't like it when I say 'boobs.' Cover your ears, Brian."

"Let's just do your blood pressure again," the nurse said.

"God must be watching all these things as they happen, right?

So it's like a TV show to him? A TV show that he doesn't really like but he doesn't turn off? Is that it?"

I had started off annoyed with my mother for fighting with the nurse, who just wanted to check her blood pressure, but I ended up kind of proud of her, and also encouraged by how well she could use her mind when she wanted to. Maybe she *was* a great logician.

The only form of therapy my sister and I felt adamant about was driver's rehabilitation. Her driving had worried us for a long time, and we didn't want to let her get behind the wheel again unless people who were trained in these matters helped her learn how to compensate for her deficits and drive carefully.

Her car had been destroyed by the flood. She said she wanted to get a new one as soon as she could.

"You can get a new car as soon as the driving teacher says it's okay."

"I don't need a driving teacher."

"I think you do."

"How can I need a driving teacher? I'm the person who taught you to drive."

"You did. And you did a great job." (She really had.)

"So how can you tell me I need a driving teacher?"

"As you get older, Mom, your reaction time slows. It happens to everybody. And you've just had a stroke. I just think you need to take a driving course. I'm really not comfortable with having you drive again if you haven't taken a course."

"Well, I'm very comfortable. I don't need a course."

"If you don't need a course, there should be no harm in taking a course."

"I'm sorry, but it's just not something I plan to do."

I got her pocketbook out of her bedside drawer, took out her wallet, and began to look through it with exaggerated gestures of curiosity, like a mime. I took each card out and examined it on one side and then the other and then put it back in.

Finally I took out the driver's license and examined it, scratching my chin.

"What's this? What's this thing for?"

My mother laughed.

"Nice picture," I said. "Reminds me of someone."

"Put that back," she said. "You nutcase."

"It seems to convey permission to operate a vehicle of some sort."

"Yes, it does. It conveys permission to drive the car I'm going to buy as soon as I get out of here."

"They say that after a certain age, humans from lessons benefit much."

Having run out of inspiration for my person-who's-never-seen-a-driver's-license-before routine, I was falling back on a Yoda impression.

"This human doesn't need a lesson. Put it back."

"Back I put it will when lesson human takes."

I put the license in my breast pocket.

"That's my property. You have no right."

She still didn't think I'd actually take it away from her, so she was still half laughing, but she was starting to become concerned.

"I really think you need to see the driving teacher."

"I really think you need to have your head examined," she said.

Soon she was released from Helen Hayes. She wasn't happy, my sister and I weren't happy, the doctors weren't happy, but Medicare would only pay for a ten-day stay, and it was hard to imagine that she'd take rehabbing more seriously even if she stayed there for a year. The discharge summary from Helen Hayes noted that "She had differences with our judgment regarding safety measures, and occasionally refused some of our routine safety interventions."

I asked her what had become of the "I'm going to do everything I need to do to get better" attitude that she'd had when she went in.

"That was before I knew they were all such meshugges in there," she said.

Before I drove to Rockland County to get her, I dropped Heather off at my mother's place in Teaneck. Heather wanted to clean up a little to make things easier for my mother when she got home.

My mother's house requires an introduction.

When their children graduate from college and begin living on their own, many couples seek a smaller and more manageable place to live. My parents, on the other hand, had moved into a long drafty Dutch Colonial built in the eighteenth century.

It was a strange house. It had many rooms, but all of them were cramped and low-ceilinged, since they were built for long-ago bodies, and everything in the place—the electricity, the plumbing, the heat—sometimes worked and sometimes didn't, either because the wiring and the pipes had been installed long ago or because they were obeying the whims of the ghosts that inhabited them. My mother had for some reason fallen in love with the house when a friend who worked in real estate took her there to look at it "just for fun," and my father had signed on to the idea—at first reluctantly, and then enthusiastically, simply because she loved it so much.

While I was picking Tasha up in Rockland County, Heather was cleaning her house. That's the wrong way to put it, though. She couldn't really clean a house in which my mother had been piling up junk for thirty-five years. She was doing what she could, establishing a few little beachheads of order and clarity within the nightmare circus that the house had become.

I've never read about the psychology of hoarding, because it never occurred to me to think of her as a hoarder. I always imagined hoarders to be orderly; when I thought of the word, I thought of someone who saves every newspaper that's ever come into their house and keeps them all in obsessively neat stacks. It wasn't until after she died that I learned there's a branch of the hoarder family who are simply slobs.

If I'd known that she could be classified as a hoarder, would it have made a difference? I would have done a lot of research, looking for a clinic or a book or a behavioral technique that could spring her from the trap of her habits. And if I'd found anything that seemed worth telling her about, she would have waved me away, saying she had everything under control.

I gave my mother my arm and we walked slowly into the house, where Heather greeted her and hugged her and helped her sit down.

Heather had been working in the kitchen. Later she and I would work together in the den, where my mother spent most of her time, but first I was going to labor alone in the dreaded downstairs bathroom.

The day before my mother went into Helen Hayes, I'd offloaded her cat to a family friend who lived in the country and had four or five cats already. I hadn't had time to deal with the cat litter. Now I went to the downstairs bathroom to take stock of the job.

The bathroom was where you found the cat litter box. For many years, my mother had had an unorthodox approach to cleaning it. Instead of dumping the contents of the box into a trash bag and throwing it out, my mother would scoop out pieces of dried excrement and slide them into the narrow blue bags in which her daily newspaper was delivered. Evidently she didn't want to spend money on conventional trash bags. One problem with this arrangement was that the newspaper bags were flimsy and thin, easily pierced by dry hard pointy pieces of cat shit. Another problem was that my mother didn't throw the bags away. She left them in the bathroom, where they attracted flies.

My mother had said that she'd be just as happy if the cat stayed with her friend in the country, so instead of cleaning the fearsome shit-encrusted box that Goody had been using for years, I just put it into a trash bag, which I sealed and put into another trash bag, which

I put into a third trash bag. I knew this was excessive but I required the multiple layers for my peace of mind. It was like when you kill a bug so big and scary and mean looking that you have to kill it again.

But my work was only beginning. Years of my mother's distinctive cat-shit-management practices had left a layer of grime across every surface of the room. I was wishing I'd had the foresight to bring a change of clothes, but it was too late to worry about that now.

Heather had brought a supply of trash bags and disinfectant wipes and plastic gloves. I put the plastic gloves on and got down on my knees and set to work.

You might ask what kind of son I was to have allowed her to live in this squalor. I asked myself that question often, and ask it still. The only answer I can find is that I'm not sure what else I could have done. You could plead with her, you could reason with her, you could send housekeepers and landscapers her way; the only thing you couldn't do was figure out how to help her. During one of her broken-bone hospital stays Heather hired a crew of three cleaning women and rented a dumpster and the five of us attacked the house together, turning it into a place that a normal person could live in, but when my mother returned she felt violated, and she remained angry for weeks—remained angry, in fact, for as long as it took for her to litter the floor with newspapers and magazines and junk mail again and leave half-eaten pieces of candy on almost every surface of almost every room.

It wasn't that much different from what it must be like to have an alcoholic parent. At some point you have to give up.

She insisted that there was only one way for us to be of help: my sister and I needed to spend time with her, going over every item in the place and deciding which to discard and which to keep.

And once I gave it a try. It was long ago. I must have been in my thirties. It was probably about ten years after my father died. I came over on a Saturday morning, prepared to spend the day helping her decide what to throw out. She sat in her easy chair and I brought a trash bag into the den and picked up things that clearly had no value, proposing to throw them away. But every time I would pick something up, she would find a reason for declaring it essential. The copy of the *New Yorker* from twenty years ago. "I haven't read it yet." A newspaper from a year ago. "I think there was something in it I need to cut out." A weather radio—a gadget she'd bought thirty years earlier from the SkyMall catalog, which received the local broadcast of the National Weather Service and nothing else. The weather radio had gotten busted long ago; it didn't work anymore; but getting rid of it was out of the question. "I'm going to get it fixed, and then I'm going to sell it. It's an antique."

Finally I put something in the trash bag without listening to her opinion. It was an old wall calendar. It wasn't filled with sentimental reminders of things she'd done: it was entirely unmarked. Nor did it feature a series of attractive pictures. It was from a bank, and the photographs that accompanied each month were photographs of the lobby.

"Why would I want to get rid of that? I can still use it."

"It's from 1983. You don't have anything you need to do in 1983."

"But the years come around again. There'll be another year with the dates and the days—you know what I mean."

I put it into the trash bag anyway. She grabbed it out and put it at her side.

"Brian! You have to show me some respect! I said I wanted your help. I didn't say I want you to bully me!"

I picked up a dusty mug that held five dusty plastic swizzle sticks. I held one of them up in the air.

"How about this? Can I throw this out? One swizzle stick. Just one."

"No!"

"Why not?"

"I can still use it. Why would I want to throw it out? There's nothing wrong with it."

"The point isn't whether you can still use it. The point is whether you need it."

"There's no reason to throw something away if I can still use it."

"What can you use it for, really? You use a swizzle stick to stir a mixed drink. When do you have mixed drinks?"

"When your father was alive, I used to make whiskey sours. Dick loved his whiskey sours."

"You haven't made a whiskey sour in years. And he won't be enjoying them anytime soon."

"I'm going to make whiskey sours again this summer, after I get the place clean. I'm going to entertain."

"But you're never going to get the place clean if you can't throw out the swizzle sticks. It's the swizzle stick paradox."

"There are plenty of other things to throw away."

"But somehow we haven't identified any of them yet! Just let me throw out one of them. I'll leave the other swizzle sticks alone. Just let me throw out this one little swizzle stick, which incidentally looks as if it may have been gnawed on by a mouse—"

I held it above the lip of the trash bag—but now she was seriously upset.

"Do not throw that away! Do not do that! This is my house! This is very disrespectful!"

(My sister, it should be noted, had always been wise enough not to argue. Once she'd tried to throw out a rotting, blackened banana, but my mother said, "I still want that! I'm going to bake banana bread." I was about to point out to my mother that she'd never made banana bread in her life and was unlikely to start now, but my sister simply put the banana down and said, "Save me a piece.")

While my argument with my mother was taking place, the remains of my father sat in noble silence on a mantel above the fireplace. My mother had never been able to bring herself to part with his ashes. Instead she'd stuffed them (still in their original plastic bag) into a samovar that they'd received as a gift during a trip to the Soviet Union the year before he died. The two of them had been ardent communists in their youth and had never entirely shed the old faith, so housing the bag of his ashes in a samovar seemed fitting, if you didn't think about it too long.

I put the swizzle stick back in the cup.

I'd never tried to help her clean the place again. Not until we brought her back from Helen Hayes.

After I'd finished cleaning the bathroom and Heather had finished the kitchen, we were too tired to take on the den, but it felt wrong to leave my mother where she was. She was sitting in an easy chair, on top of books and cookies.

"Mom. How can you stay here?"

"It's fine. I'll be fine."

"But you're going to slip and hurt yourself again."

"I'm going to clean up. I'll do a little every day. I was already getting somewhere when I got sick. I'm making progress. You'll see."

I was frustrated with her, frustrated with myself. She had proven again and again that she couldn't take care of herself, and now that she'd had a stroke it was only going to get worse. And yet here I was, doing nothing. It wasn't because I didn't want to. It was because I didn't know what to do.

She'd been living like this since 1984. My father had come home late from work one night, said that he had a funny story to tell her but that he was tired and would tell her in the morning, and gone up to bed. By the time she joined him, he was asleep. In the morning, she woke when her alarm went off, and, surprised that he was still in bed, said, "Now what was that story?" and reached out to give him a playful push. As soon as she touched him, she knew he was gone.

Dying in your sleep without having been ill—that's probably the ideal way to die, for the person who does the dying. But for everyone else, it's unspeakable. The mind can't fathom it. For months I dreamed that my father had died but was waiting around to die again: in my dream universe, you had to die a second time in order to be truly gone. He'd be sitting in the kitchen, grayed out, drinking coffee, and I'd feel lucky to be with him, but also desolate, because I knew what was ahead.

The day he died I heard her talking to herself. "The dominant figure in my life is gone," she said.

She was inconsolable during the year that followed, and of course I understood this—so was I. When she remained grief-stricken through the year after that, I simply thought that after a great loss, people come back to life in their own time. But I'm not sure she ever really did.

She stopped teaching—although she'd determined that she could afford to stop, what with her pension and his Social Security, it still seemed a questionable choice—and thereafter had little structure in her life. She went to her board of ed meetings, but apart from that she had no obligations anymore. She would sleep till one in the afternoon and wake up feeling defeated, convinced that it was already too late to make a mark on the day.

She was still a woman of stubborn energy, but somehow she could no longer use it to reach toward a wider life. Instead she seemed to turn it against herself, as if she were fighting to hold on to her incapacities.

This is when the hoarding began. Soon every room in her house was like a cry for help.

When Heather was cleaning the refrigerator she found some gherkins that might have been there for thirty-five years. They were no longer recognizable as gherkins; you could identify them only from the label on the jar. I showed my mother the jar and raised my eyebrows.

"Dick loved gherkins," she said.

When we were about to leave, my mother suggested that Heather and I take a little walk before driving home.

"There's nothing like springtime in Teaneck," my mother said.

Heather had grown up in the Bay Area, within view of Mount Tamalpais, a short drive from the thousand-year-old redwoods in Muir Woods.

"I'm not sure anyone's ever said that exact sentence before," she said.

"Are you crazy?" my mother said.

Such were her feelings about Teaneck.

Teaneck is a town in Bergen Country, New Jersey, about five miles from the George Washington Bridge, convenient for people who work in the city but don't want to live there. (When I was little and first heard it called a "bedroom community," I was indignant on Teaneck's behalf.)

It's an odd place, because it can plausibly be viewed as the ultimate in suburban blandness or as an emblem of some of our best traditions. In the 1960s it became the first locality in the United States to use busing to integrate its schools—the first to do this voluntarily, as the result of a democratic election, rather than because of a court order. When I was little I assumed that Teaneck was a microcosm of the country as a whole, and I was astonished when I found out that America wasn't mostly Jewish and Black.

My mother seemed to love everything about the place: the preference for integration; the anti-redlining group; the forward-looking school system; the placid downtown area, with its one bagel store, its one ice cream parlor, and its one bookstore. In the early 1990s, during a period when race relations in Teaneck seemed to be going backward, she attended every one of the earnest town meetings set up for people in the community to talk it all through. She'd had plans to visit friends on the Jersey Shore that summer, but she canceled them, because the meetings were so important to her. She was a patriot of Teaneck.

In later years Teaneck became a dream community for Orthodox Jews. I don't know why it happened; I don't know if there were any particular sociological dynamics that made the town uniquely appealing; but by the beginning of the twenty-first century, there were about twenty Orthodox synagogues in Teaneck's six square miles. On Saturday afternoons you had to drive slowly, mindful of the Orthodox families walking down the middle of the street on their way home from shul. They were walking because they were observing the Sabbath, and they were walking down the middle of the street because . . . I don't actually know why they were walking down the middle of the street.

My mother found them radically annoying. This was something she could pass off as a matter of political principle, in view of the fact that they didn't send their kids to public schools and they voted against increasing the school budgets. But in truth her feelings about them were independent of local politics. When I was little and we visited relatives in Brooklyn, my mother would always point out the Orthodox with a kind of mocking incredulity. "Look at those payess! Look at those hats! Do they know what century they're in?"

I never wondered why she felt this way. It was just one of her prejudices, like the one that made her sure that only an idiot could like angel food cake. This was a passionately held belief. Once she took Melinda and me along when she visited one of her best friends, a woman named Nancy. Melinda and I had been playing in the living room for about five minutes when my mother appeared and told us we were going home. Evidently Nancy had pulled an angel food cake out of the oven and my mother had denounced it with her customary fervor. The normally forbearing Nancy had fought back, and they'd been standing in the kitchen toe to toe, exchanging insults. Before we had time to get to the car, though, my mother and Nancy, on the front porch, were crying in each other's arms. The battle of the angel food cake had ended in a beautiful truce.

Once when I was home on a break from college, I tried to talk her out of her feelings about the Orthodox, pointing out that she disliked most religions because of their intolerance, and it was therefore contradictory to—

She told me not to waste my breath.

Anyway, that was Teaneck.

Within days of being back at home, my mother was talking about buying a new car. The discharge summary said that "She was told she was not currently cleared to drive due to dizziness and decreased attention," but this carried no legal force. Things would have been simpler if it had.

"We've already gone over this," I said. "I'll give you your license back when you do the rehab thing."

"I'm not going to do the rehab thing. Just give it back. You have no right to hold on to it."

We had this conversation every time we talked. I don't know why she refused to do the rehab thing. I don't know if it was pride that held her back, or fear—fear that if she took a course, she wouldn't pass it.

She persuaded a friend to take her to a car rental office. She came with an expired license, her ID card from her days as a teacher, a library card, a Medicare card, two credit cards, and a newspaper article about her many years on the board of education.

When her friend told me about this, I wondered, as I'd wondered before, how much her thinking had been disordered by the stroke. Was this something she might have done two years ago— think she had a shot at getting the car rental guy to let her have a car on the strength of a newspaper article and a library card?

If you lose your license, or if your son takes it away from you,

you can get a new one, but in order to do so, you need to go to the DMV with your passport or birth certificate. But her passport was expired and she couldn't find her birth certificate. Getting a new one would have required a trip to the Bureau of Vital Records in Manhattan, and she couldn't manage a trip of this complexity on her own—in fact, I don't think she was even capable of figuring out that she could have gotten a new one this way. Her son had taken her driver's license and he wouldn't give it back: this, I think, represented the limits of her understanding.

After the blow of finding that she couldn't rent a car with her library card, all she would talk about with me was how cruel I was.

"I thought you were a really good person. But this isn't something a good person does. This is evil. I have no place I can go. I have to stay home all day."

"You don't have to stay home all day. Most of the places you want to go to are within a five-mile radius. There are three different taxi companies in Teaneck. You can take a taxi."

"I've never taken a taxi in my life and I'm not going to start taking taxis now."

"What could be wrong with taking a taxi?"

"Pay someone to drive me somewhere? I don't need to pay anyone to drive me anywhere. I'm a very good driver. I'm a better driver than anybody who drives a cab."

At the time I was frustrated by my mother's self-delusions: her delusion that she was making progress with the house; her delusion that the reason she couldn't hear people was that nobody knew how to speak up anymore; her delusion that there was nothing wrong with her driving, and that all the dings and scrapes and scratches she'd accumulated during the last few years were caused by other people's carelessness.

But thinking about it now, I can see that my own delusions were just as strong. I was sure that she could find the will to change. During the first few weeks after her stroke, when she was so surprisingly accepting of our help, I thought she was going to do everything she could to turn her life around. Now I can see how naive I was, both about her and about human nature. Even when you're fully committed to changing your life, changing your life is so, so hard.

When had she given me the idea that she was ready to do the hard work of change? Apart from the declarations she'd made when Heather and I were driving her up to Helen Hayes, I don't think she had. I'd wished the idea into existence.

Meanwhile, she was refusing to take a cab, because she was a better driver than any cabbie.

Here is one of my illusions in detail. I had called all three cab companies in Teaneck and ascertained that it would be possible for me to set up an account with any of them so that my mother would never have to pay for her rides. I imagined she might develop a relationship with a cabbie. I imagined something heartwarming, something out of a movie, in which the cabbie, a hardworking Palestinian immigrant, and the passenger, a cantankerous Jewish communist, at first regard each other suspiciously, then rail at each other in a sharp-tongued but good-natured way, and finally come to mean more to each other than anyone would have believed possible.

I'm putting it in a caricatured form, but I really did wish for something like this. I not only wished for it—I came close to expecting it.

It wasn't a totally crazy thing to wish for. My mother loved to talk to strangers. When I lived in the city, my mother, when she visited, would strike up conversations in the elevator with people I'd been encountering for years and with whom I'd never exchanged a word. Grandparents, parents, children; white, black, brown: she was an equal opportunity schmoozer, feeling free to offer her opinions to anyone who crossed her path. She never, for example, hesitated to tell someone what they were doing wrong, from a businessman who was holding his umbrella in a way that risked jabbing other people to a kid who was wiping his nose on his hand instead of using a tissue. And no one ever got mad at her for it.

So if I was under the illusion that she might develop a relationship of affectionate raillery with some cabdriver and come to love taking cabs around town, it wasn't an illusion that had no basis in the possible.

And if I kept hoping she'd find a way to make the best of a bad situation, that wasn't dreamed up out of nowhere either. When I was a kid, she was always making the best of bad situations. It was almost an art form. We were poor when I was growing up, but it never felt like we were poor. We had a couch that was old and falling apart; when two of its legs broke, she removed the other two, and, telling us about the Japanese custom of sitting on the floor, began calling it "the Japanese couch." It was years before I realized that she and my father hadn't replaced the couch because they couldn't afford to.

When I was in kindergarten I came home from school one day to find my mother in an excited mood. She told my sister and me that we were in for a treat. We were going to visit our grandparents in Pittsburgh! And we were going today!

I loved my grandparents, and they were fun—or at any rate, my grandfather was fun, and the two of them liked to buy toys for me, so this was thrilling. My mother drove us all the way to Pittsburgh—it was bedtime by the time we arrived—and drove back the same night, and my sister and I stayed there for a week. During the next few days I watched a Davy Crockett movie on TV—it was the first time I heard about his famous coonskin cap—and read a book about Francis Marion (the "Swamp Fox"), and on a trip to the supermarket my grandmother bought me a pack of plastic toy soldiers, little green guys, whose features I remember to this day. The trip still glows in my memory.

I learned only many years later that my parents' marriage was at a low point, and that they needed to get us out of the way so they could figure out if they were going to stay together. I learned this from my mother, years after my father died. She said he'd lost his job and had been too proud to admit it—for weeks he'd been leaving the house and going to the library, pretending to be at work—and that she'd discovered this only when she was dusting the bookshelf and found an unemployment check pressed between two books. She said that when she asked him about it, embarrassment quickly hardened into anger, and he barely spoke to her for weeks.

Parts of the story struck me as a little fishy: it was impossible to imagine my mother dusting a bookshelf. But it wasn't hard to imagine him turning stonily remote.

She told me that during one of their conversations that weekend, he cried, saying that he didn't want to live without his children, and that it was one of the only two times she saw him cry, the other being when his mother died.

He didn't want to live without his children. When she told me this, she didn't say it with any bitterness; she seemed to be remembering it as a moving, beautiful thing to say. It doesn't sound beautiful to me. I wish he'd told her that he couldn't live without *her*.

(The cold anger, the weeks of silence, the avowal of his desire to stay married to her that didn't seem to be about her at all—why did she put up with it? Why didn't she ask for more? She was a feminist at a time when no one was using the word; both of them were political radicals, devoted to questioning all existing social arrangements; but they were also people of their time, trapped in the assumptions of their time, which didn't provide much room for men to be human beings. My father didn't like to drive, and my mother once told me a story about the early days of their marriage, in which they picked up a friend at the airport and he pretended to have a wrist injury to account for why she, not he, was driving. It's hard for me to imagine being confined by an idea of masculinity so rigid that it would have been humiliating to admit that your wife was a better driver than you. But maybe I'm confined by notions as rigid as this, and just can't see them.)

The trip to Pittsburgh—the unexpectedness, the joy—left a

permanent mark on me. It left me with the belief that even on the most ordinary day, there's a chance of a fantastic surprise.

One of my favorite essayists, Albert Murray, often says that the willingness to improvise is at the heart of any well-lived life. In her younger years my mother knew how to improvise. It was hard to give up the hope that she'd find that skill again.

In the weeks after her stroke, while she was confined to her house—confined by my refusal to give her back her license, her refusal to call a cab—many of her friends decided to disappear.

Alongside the dream of the Palestinian cabbie, I'd dreamed that her friends might form a sort of emotional bucket brigade. I imagined them teaming up to take her to board of ed meetings once a week; I daydreamed that they'd put together a "let's help Tasha" calendar, so that all of them did a little bit for her and no one had to do too much. She had so many friends, I thought, that if each of them had her over to dinner just once every two months, she'd have a satisfying social life. But somehow almost all of them, as they say in spy novels, went dark.

Her friend Isabel (not her real name), both of whose children had been students of my mother's, who'd been a fixture in my mother's life for decades, who'd told me, in an emotional conversation just after my mother suffered her stroke, how much she loved her and how much she owed her, decided, once my mother became housebound, to stop returning her calls. Her friend Lynn (not hers either), whose *three* children had been my mother's students, and whom she'd known since 1971, ran an annual auction to raise money for the school system, which my mother had attended faithfully every year, making donations and serving as a volunteer. (Her favorite volunteer job was ticket taker, but Lynn had switched her to the envelope-stuffing team because my mother liked to chat with everyone whose ticket she punched, holding up the line so badly that the bidding couldn't start on time.) When my mother received an email invitation to the fall 2010 auction, she wrote to Lynn: "I'd really love to come, but I don't have a car anymore." The translation of this, clearly, was: "Maybe you can find a volunteer to pick me up? Maybe you can pick me up yourself?" Lynn's reply was simply "That's too bad."

It's easy to become an injustice collector after a loved one dies, and I'm aware that I might sound like one. Often I tried to tell myself that I shouldn't be so indignant about the way her friends had disappeared. Everybody's busy; everybody has their life. But after she died, both Isabel and Lynn approached me at the memorial service, separately and unprompted, to say they regretted not having been better to her during her last years. Isabel even cried. Because charity seemed preferable to bitterness, I did my best to absolve them, telling them I understood that they had a lot of demands on their time. But now I wonder whether it wouldn't have been better to be honest and to remind them that life gives us only a limited number of chances to be the people we want to be, and that when they were called, they hadn't answered.

I sometimes thought about her friends' disappearance with a kind of zoological curiosity. Maybe this is just what certain animals do when one of their kind is dying.

But that can't be it. We all know people who've been better than that.

When I find myself thinking I have the right to judge her

friends, I try to remember that I need to judge myself as well. Although I dreamed that all her friends would band together to help her, I didn't ask them to. I hinted; I wrote them group emails with specific questions (asking for recommendations for plumbers and electricians and other people to take care of her house), but I never asked them for the kind of help I was hoping they'd give. It doesn't really make sense for me to be angry that they didn't give it.

My failure to ask is of a piece with who I am. I don't like to ask for things. But I should have understood that whatever imagined nobility there is in not asking for anything for oneself, there's no nobility at all in not asking for anything for others.

And then a touch of compassion and community came from an unexpected direction.

In the year or two before her stroke, she'd been going occasionally to the seniors' center at an Orthodox synagogue in Teaneck. At first she went there only for the inexpensive lunches. She'd get a chicken sandwich and a container of pudding, eat half the sandwich, wrap the other half in a napkin, and take the half a sandwich and the pudding home for dinner. She loved a bargain, and she loved to feel like she was getting away with something—"tricking the world," as she used to put it—so this made her doubly happy.

The seniors' center had a jitney service for members who didn't drive. It was free, so she was happy to use it, and it meant that she could get out of the house while maintaining her proud unbroken record of never having paid for a cab. Soon she was going to the center every day.

"Who would have thought I'd end up spending all my time in a synagogue?" she would say. "I'm the most anti-religious person I know."

What had merely been a source of inexpensive food became a social world. She complained about it all the time—the daily bingo was beneath her, the other women there were yentas and yekkes—but she never missed a day. Sometimes the mayor or another local notable would drop by. Sometimes theater students from Fairleigh

Dickinson, the university down the road, would give a lunchtime performance. Occasionally a group of schoolchildren would visit to do art projects with the seniors. I think she liked these visits most of all. She loved to tell them that when she was a teacher, she had a phone in her classroom, which she used for educational purposes, teaching phone manners to her students. Every day a different child would be assigned the formidable task of answering the phone with the words, "Children's Phone. May I help you, please?"

It really was a lovely idea, the Children's Phone. Having a telephone in the classroom and being entrusted with the responsibility of answering it: this made her five- and six-year-olds feel grownup, at the same time as it meant their parents were never out of reach.

Once I dropped in on her classroom on the opening day of the school year, just as the first graders were demonstrating the Children's Phone to the kindergartners. The first graders were smoothly confident, and the kindergartners seemed to be in awe. The expression on some of the new kids' faces was something to behold.

A few times a week, the rabbi visited the seniors' center, sometimes to give a little talk, sometimes just to say hello. He was an energetic man in his forties, articulate, learned, a little scattered. When he was struck by an idea for one of his sermons he'd write it down on a scrap of paper, and later he would lose it. Almost all of his sermons were improvised.

He liked to tease her about her atheism. "The Orthodox aren't so bad, are we, Tasha?" Soon she had a crush on him.

She never relented in her distaste for religion, but she could recognize kindness when she saw it.

After Saturday morning services, the rabbi always gave a lecture on some ethical or philosophical topic, which was accompanied by a buffet lunch. My mother became a regular. She could never tell me what the lectures were about, but for someone who'd been around education and ideas all her life, the weekly gatherings brought both comfort and excitement.

On Saturdays, there was no jitney service. Which leads me to another bright spot in her life. At the same time as her friends were mysteriously vanishing, one person came forward to help. His name was Sigismund Laster—Siggy. This is one real name I'll use. He was a member of the synagogue and a Good Samaritan. When other members were in the hospital, Siggy would visit; when anyone needed transportation anywhere—to doctors, to supermarkets—Siggy would drive them. Now he took it upon himself to drive my mother to and from the synagogue every Saturday. Of course he wasn't supposed to drive on the Sabbath, but he believed the injunction to help others was higher than the injunction to follow the laws.

He didn't ask for compensation; he didn't ask for anything. He didn't seem to regard what he was doing as special in any way.

Jewish tradition has it that at any given time, there are thirty-six righteous men—just, loyal, humble—on whom the fate of the world depends. No one knows who they are. They themselves don't know. I used to suspect that if the story of the thirty-six men were true, then Siggy was among them.

By taking away her car, I'd taken away her social role. Instead of bustling around town, a voluble and energetic eighty-five-year-old, she was stuck in her house. If you wanted to be dramatic about it, you could call it a social death.

But now she'd found a new role. It wasn't as satisfying as her old ones, but it was a social role nevertheless. She loved listening to the rabbi's lectures. Sometimes she even came early, to attend the services. She loved helping the aides serve lunch (though I heard from the seniors' center director that my mother's style of helping usually made the aides' jobs harder). She loved feeling superior to the women who played bingo. Many of the members of the seniors' center community drove her nuts, but she was grateful to have a community to be driven nuts by.

She even forgave me for taking away her driver's license. At least she stopped telling me that it was the cruelest thing anyone had ever done to her. That may not quite have been forgiveness, but it was close enough.

My younger son, Gabriel, was turning eight in February 2011. He wanted to have an outdoor party, with snowball fights and s'mores, and Heather and I decided to hold it on the campus of Sarah Lawrence, where I teach.

I told my mother that he was having a snowball-fight party and that we'd like to take her out to dinner to celebrate his birthday the next day.

She said, "I'll do both."

"It wouldn't make sense for you to come to the party. It'll be slippery. It'll be cold. The kids are going to be running around. It won't be fun for you. Let's just go out to a nice dinner the next day."

"The next day won't be his birthday."

"That's true. But we can *celebrate* his birthday the next day."

"So you don't want me to see my grandson on his birthday."

"It's not that I don't want you to see your grandson on his birthday. It's that what we're doing on his birthday would be uncomfortable and dangerous for you, and I'm sure it would be a drag for you, and it would be a drag for me to be worrying about you the whole time, and it would be much better for everyone if we could get together in a nice warm cozy restaurant the next day."

"Then just forget it. If I can't see my grandson on his birthday then you don't have to put up with me at all. That's fine."

I can't remember the rest of the conversation, or the other

conversations we had about it that week. In particular, I can't remember when I said okay, you can come if you want.

Why did I change my mind?

Why did I say yes?

It's possible that someone interceded with me. It's possible that Heather suggested a compromise that would enable my mother to attend while keeping her safe and out of everyone's hair. It's possible that Emmett, who was ten, was the one who spoke up—Emmett had always been a genius at finding compromises that worked for everyone. It's possible that Gabe himself expressed a desire for her to be there.

It would be nice to think that one of these things happened. It would be nice to think that I didn't just give up in the face of my mother's insistence. But either way, the decision was mine.

I think I could write the history of being my mother's son as a history of ill-considered yesses. It took years for me to understand that some of the things she asked of her children were not quite reasonable, and years after that to understand that when she asked for too much, I had the right to say no. If you're brought up to be a "good boy," it can take the better part of a lifetime to learn that you don't actually always have to be so damn good.

Over the years I'd become better at not responding with an unthinking stupid yes to almost anything she asked of me. But now that she was so frail and so compromised, and now that I bore the responsibility for having taken her license away, it had again become difficult to guard against the automatic yes.

We drove out to Teaneck to get her and then brought her back up to Westchester. Heather and I had arranged for one of my former students, an empathetic young woman named Naomi, who was now one of the kids' babysitters, to spend the afternoon with her in the school café.

But when we got there and I told my mother the plan, she recoiled.

"I'm not going to sit there talking with somebody I don't know. No sirree. I'm going to the party."

"The ground is covered with ice, Mom. You could hurt yourself."

"You're going to the party, aren't you? You could hurt yourself too. Why don't *you* stay inside having tea and being treated like an invalid?"

Because I'm not fucking eighty-six years old, I was on the verge of saying.

Heather read my expression and knew, more or less, what I was going to say.

"Let's talk for a minute, Tash," she said, and took my mother's arm, and they went off together toward the café.

I knew that things would be all right. Even at her grumpiest, it was impossible for my mother to sustain a bad mood after Heather had decided to charm her out of it.

I'd met Heather when she was a student in a class I was teaching in the MFA writing program at NYU. (She was in her thirties, I was in my forties, and I didn't ask her out until the summer, after the class had ended. If this nevertheless strikes you as morally questionable, I congratulate you on the simplicity of your life.)

In class she had struck me as almost shockingly alive. There never seemed to be a moment when she wasn't fully alert, fully *there*. She reminded me—this is going to sound ridiculous—she reminded me, in a spiritual sense, of Keith Hernandez. When Hernandez played for the Mets in the mid-1980s, you would watch him at first base as every pitch was thrown, and the sheer intensity of his attention to the moment was like a lesson in how to live.

One evening when Heather and I had just begun to see each other, I'd joined her at the Empire State Building to meet friends of hers who were in from California along with their three boys. They wanted to see the city from the observation deck.

It was a humid day in July, the line was long, and the air-conditioning wasn't working. We stood in the lobby for an hour. Everyone was showing their annoyance, with gestures that probably only made them feel worse: fanning themselves, sighing, looking at their watches (this was before phones), shifting with theatrical boredom from hip to hip. Everyone was fed up—everyone, it seemed, but Heather. I'm sure she wasn't enjoying the heat and the crowd any more than anyone else was, but somehow she was keeping it all in perspective, seeing the inconveniences as small compared to the pleasure of being with people she cared about.

Whatever quality it was that kept her buoyant was mystifying to me—I was one of the people checking their watches—but I wanted to learn more about it. I wanted to be around it. I wanted to be around her.

Now Heather exited the café alone and gave me a thumbs-up.

"She's fine," Heather said. "I got her some candy and she

cheered right up. Naomi showed up a couple of minutes ago, and they're having a jolly time."

Naomi sat and talked with my mother, more or less interviewing her, for two hours. I would go out and participate in the activities, puzzled by one father who was throwing snowballs much too hard, and then go back and check on my mother, who, it turned out, was flowering under Naomi's attention.

Is it too pop-psychology-ish of me to say that this was the key to most of her problems—that she could never get enough attention? Her father was an artist, an egotist, and the life of the party—even when I knew him, he was a man in perpetual motion, brimming with gifts, jokes, stories, filling your life with little adventures—who was always on the lam from his family. In the 1930s he was an actor and director in the Yiddish theater in New York. After the Yiddish theater died out (killed off, you could say, by the movies and the Holocaust), he became an itinerant artist, traveling to Milwaukee, to Montreal, to Los Angeles, to Pittsburgh, becoming the artistic director of the theater programs at Jewish centers in each city. This too is a vanished world, one in which there was so much support for the arts that Jewish centers could have theater programs through which people were able to earn a living. Who can imagine such a thing today?

My grandfather, Chaim, would get a job at one of these places and go off there by himself; after a few months my grandmother, Leah, would take both children and follow him. (My mother had an older brother named Heskel, a musical prodigy from whom everyone expected great things.) They would all live together for a year or so, and then my grandfather would hear the highway calling (is that the right expression? Can Jewish men be said to hear the highway calling?), and he'd move on, finding another job in another part of the continent, and after a few months my grandmother would pack up both children and follow him again.

Part of what was going on was that Chaim had what at the time would have been called a mistress, a woman named Amelia. Amelia would join him in each new city, and when my grandmother arrived, Amelia would return to the Bronx.

His relationship with Amelia lasted until his death. One of the oddities of it all was that my sister and I knew Amelia and knew that he sometimes lived with her. In the 1960s, my grandparents spent a year in Israel; when they returned, just after the Six-Day War, Chaim preceded Leah by a few months and stayed with Amelia in her apartment. This didn't seem strange to me, because no one treated it as strange. You grow up within the culture of your family, and you believe that the way things are done within this culture is simply the way things are done.

I vastly preferred Amelia to my grandmother. For one thing, she wasn't always trying to kiss me. My grandmother's kisses were fat and sloppy and weirdly violent, and, forever pressuring you to eat her gefilte fish and her matzoh ball soup and her kasha, she seemed like someone who had just stepped out of the shtetl. Amelia was reserved and watchful and ironic, and she seemed like someone who belonged in the modern world. She could work the television. She could work a push-button telephone. She knew who the Monkees were.

Whenever my grandfather escaped again and Tasha (six years old, eight, ten, twelve) was left alone with her mother and brother, she had a rough time. Even decades later, even to me, it was clear that Heskel was the undisputed apple of their mother's eye. The anecdote about Tasha's early life that stays with me is that there was a piano in their apartment in the Bronx, but she wasn't allowed to touch it, because it was for Heskel and Heskel alone.

You could say that my mother's formative experience in life was worshipping a father who was always running away. And you could say that what came of that was an adult life in which she was always trying to prevent everybody from leaving. And maybe you could even say that that was why she couldn't get rid of anything. Not even a swizzle stick.

When the birthday party was over, I went to the café, thanked Naomi, took my mother's arm, and walked her to the car to drive her home. When she was at the passenger door, I let go of her for a moment so I could put something into the trunk. I don't know why I did that. I don't know why I didn't get her into the car first.

She moved one of her feet, slipped, and went face-first onto the pavement.

I helped her up, struggling to maintain my own balance on the icy road. It was as if the two of us were on roller skates.

Her nose was bloody, her arms were scraped, and she was trembling.

Heather went back to the café and ran warm water over some paper towels. Then she came back and cleaned my mother's face.

I drove her back to her house in a fever of rage at myself and a slightly lower fever of rage at her. Why had I fucked up? Why had I fucked up at the very last minute, when everything before that had so improbably gone so well? And why had I let her whine her way into joining this fucking party in the first place? Why hadn't I just fucking said no?

When I called her the next day, she was the one who was furious, because I hadn't called to check on her the night before.

"I hurt myself very badly. I had a headache all night. You saw that I hurt myself. But you didn't call. Why didn't you call?"

"I'm sorry," I said.

I hadn't called because I'd been too angry—at her, at myself. But now I knew I'd fucked up. It's not just that I should have called her. I shouldn't have let her go home.

When you're growing up and your parents are annoying you, you can try to ignore them. If you're good at living in the world of your imagination, you can pretend, for long periods of time, that they don't even exist.

This, obviously, isn't something you can do with your children. No matter how angry you are at your children, you have to make sure they're safe.

I'd known that my mother had reached a point where she had to be treated like a child in this sense, and that I needed to look out for her even when I found her maddening. But I'd been so irritated that I'd forgotten.

When I was in college, still in my teens, a teacher once mentioned that he'd recently gone into therapy to work out some unresolved feelings about his parents. I didn't say anything, but I remember being aghast. Not aghast, but scornful. *You're still trying to work out your stuff with your parents! Does it ever end! Christ, you must be thirty years old!*

And here I was, at sixty.

I want to finish the story of Amelia, my grandfather's lover, or girlfriend, or mistress—none of the words in our vocabulary feels quite right.

My grandmother died in the fall of 1974, a few days after Rosh Hashanah. I wondered whether my grandfather would move in with Amelia, or whether she'd lose her appeal for him now that he no longer had Leah to run away from. But he was diagnosed with lung cancer just a few weeks later and was gone himself before the end of the year.

It was one of life's ironies that after his death and the death of Amelia's brother a few years later, my mother, who'd always loathed and resented her, became the only person Amelia had left. When Amelia couldn't live on her own anymore, my mother secured a place for her in the Actors Home, an affordable assisted living facility for former artists and entertainers, and visited her every week until she died.

I said it was "one of life's ironies," and that's the way I'd always thought of it. It's only in writing about it now that I realize that I've always missed the point. The point of the story isn't that life strangely put her in the position of having to care for Amelia. The point is that it was a responsibility she could have easily sidestepped, but she decided, because she was the person she was, to take it on.

In earlier days, writers loved nothing more than issuing manifestos. If you had an idea, you couldn't just communicate it; you had to issue a manifesto and proclaim it. You had to act as if you thought the world would be transformed if everybody else believed it too.

If this were a different time, I'd be writing a manifesto to declare that men need to learn to identify with their mothers, in order to foster the capacity for nurturing that most of us leave undeveloped. I'd claim that men need to acknowledge how much we take from our mothers if the world is to have any chance of being healed.

It's easy for a man to acknowledge his spiritual debt to his father. It's easy for a man to look in the mirror and see the ghost of his father there.

Easy for a man to think: I *am* my father.

I am my mother is more difficult.

(I'm aware, by the way, that my generalizations may be nothing more than artifacts of an era that's already passed, symptoms of a personality type that's vanishing along with the historical moment that produced it. Maybe my beliefs and assumptions are merely those of someone born in the emotional frigidity of the 1950s.)

But *why* is it more difficult for a man to identify with his mother?

You don't have to be a Freudian to think that as a boy grows up, he'll tend to model himself on his father. And that he'll test himself against his father, in a thousand ways. And that eventually, he'll dream about outdistancing him.

Precisely because we've struggled against our fathers, men end up understanding how much we owe to them. The struggle shows us what we share.

I don't know why, but we don't struggle with our mothers in the same way. And in failing to struggle with them, we fail to learn how much they shaped us.

Your father is to be confronted; your mother is to be escaped.

Part of the reason I'm writing about Tasha is that I don't want to remain oblivious. I want to acknowledge a depth of connection that it was hard for me to acknowledge when she was alive.

But even as I express these thoughts, I recoil from them. I'm not sure I *want* to be a man who identifies with his mother!

Whether I like it or not, I *am* the product of a different time.

When I was in junior high school, I used to binge-read the great private eye novels, dreaming that I was Raymond Chandler's Philip Marlowe or Dashiell Hammett's Continental Op. When I think about where I got my idea of manhood, I think about these books.

Would you ever catch Philip Marlowe identifying with his mother? Or the Continental Op? Never! They followed the clues, made a few wisecracks, got beaten up a little, figured out that all the suspects were in it together, turned everybody in to the police, and went home. They didn't sit around thinking about their mothers. They never even mentioned them.

A few years ago, I revisited my love of the great private detectives when I came upon Robert B. Parker's Spenser novels. Spenser is an updated version of the classic private eye: he's as handy with his fists as any of the gumshoes of old, but he maintains a loving long-term relationship, he's in touch with his feelings, and he knows how to cook.

Unlike Philip Marlowe or the Continental Op, Spenser does mention his mother. But only once. And he mentions her only to tell us that she died while she was carrying him and that he was delivered through a cesarean. As another character says, he was "not of woman born." That's all we learn about her, in a series that spanned forty books.

The lesson is clear: tough guys don't write about their mothers.

I seem to have wandered away from my "Guys, We Need to Think More About What We Took from Our Mothers" manifesto.

Do I really believe the world could be healed if men acknowledged how much they take from their mothers? I don't. Orwell has warned us of the intellectual limitations of the "change-of-heart man," who believes that things would be fine if we looked inside ourselves and made psychological adjustments. As Tasha would be the first to say, politics requires collective action.

But then again, collective action will never get us where we want to go—to a world that's more fair, more generous, more respectful of nature, a world in which we share what we have—if we *don't* look inside ourselves and make changes. Maybe I'll stand behind my manifesto after all.

A week or two after Gabe's birthday party, on the phone, my mother mentioned that she was planning to see her doctor, to check up on "that thing I had."

"Which thing? You've had a lot of things."

"That thing I had that Melinda also had."

"What thing?"

"Emmett had it too, I think. That thing where you get the cells."

"Are you talking about a bone marrow transplant?"

"I think so."

"Emmett had a transplant, and Melinda had a transplant. You never had a transplant."

"I think I did."

"You had cancer, Mom, twenty years ago. And you had chemo and radiation. You never had a bone marrow transplant."

"I'm pretty sure I did," she said.

This was something new. Before this, she'd sometimes been confused about when something had happened or unable to find a word she was looking for, but this seemed like a different order of confusion. I hoped it was a momentary lapse rather than a prelude to anything lasting.

In a phone call a few days later, she said, "Do I give you and Melinda money?"

"Yes, you do. You put a hundred and eighty dollars a month into each of the kids' college funds."

She was generous with us, and it helped.

Her gifts were almost always in multiples of eighteen. In Hebrew, the number is associated with the word *chai*, the word that means "life."

"How do I do it? Do I send you a check every month?"

"It's automatic. You do it through the credit union."

For years her relationship with the Teaneck teachers' credit union was one of those small recurring pleasures that our lives, if we're lucky, are filled with. She liked the women who worked there; she enjoyed dropping by and chatting with them. She hadn't been able to do that for almost a year, ever since I, briefly the cruelest person in the world, had taken her license, but nevertheless I was surprised it had disappeared from her memory.

She laughed.

"I don't remember too many things anymore."

"Does it bother you?"

"What do I need it all for?"

She didn't need the math required for cooking a turkey; she didn't need to remember the credit union. The way she was taking all this was a relief.

A week later, Heather and the kids and I drove to Teaneck to take her out to dinner, along with my sister, her husband Mike, and their two kids, Matt and Marisa.

It was rare that all of us got together, and it wasn't easy for her. On the one hand, it was what she claimed to want more than anything: togetherness with her children and their families. On the other hand, what she claimed to want more than anything was never what she hoped it would be. (Old story, I know.)

The restaurant was noisy, so she couldn't hear what anyone was saying, and even when she could, it was hard for her to follow. She could follow a story along a slow, straight path, but if it took a turn, it lost her. She kept asking us to repeat ourselves, and when we did repeat ourselves, she kept not understanding what we'd said.

We tried to compensate by keeping the focus on her, but this wasn't easy either. After half a glass of wine, she lost her ability to tell stories; all she could do was repeat the few phrases that had become her touchstones. Whenever someone mentioned her life as a teacher, she would say, "Children's Phone. May I help you please?" If the conversation turned to my father, she would say he had a story he'd said he'd tell her in the morning. Then she would give a sad, helpless shrug.

By the time the entrées arrived, her head was drooping. Her forehead was close to the table. I thought she was asleep but, without lifting her head, she said, "It's hot in here. Why is it so hot in here?"

When the waiter came by, she struggled upright and said to him, "Could you turn the weather down?"

My niece, Marisa, was becoming agitated.

"What's wrong with Mima?" she said to my sister, in a voice loud enough for everyone but my mother to hear.

When my mother picked up her wineglass again, Marisa said, "Why don't you stop her?" She was speaking to my sister, but I think she was appealing to all of us, all the grown-ups. And I think what she was asking was, "Why can't you stop what's happening to her?"

"It's so hot in here," my mother said. "They should turn the weather down." Then she began to sing: "Turn the weather down, boys, turn the weather down." It was like a sea shanty.

"I don't think we should let her stay by herself tonight," Heather said.

A memory did come to my mother.

"I told my papa I wanted to be an actor, just like him, but he told me I couldn't, because I couldn't carry a tune."

You're still trying to work out your stuff with your parents! Does it ever end!

After the meal, we told my mother that we were taking her with us to Westchester.

"I don't want to go to Westchester," my mother said. "Westchester is for wimps. I want to go home."

"It's just for the night. We'll drive you back first thing in the morning."

"You have no right."

"We just want to make sure you're safe tonight."

"You have no right to take me away from my home. It's a kidnapping!"

"Come on, Mom."

I started to lead her out to the car.

She turned back toward the restaurant and shouted, "I'm being kidnapped!"

Some of the people at the nearby tables looked up. I thought of trying to explain what was happening, but while I was trying to find the words, I saw that everyone had already turned away again.

My children looked worried and confused. Heather knelt beside them to explain what was going on.

After we got her into the car, she was still howling.

"I want to go home! I want to go home!"

Surely she will stop this soon, I thought as I turned the key in the ignition.

But she was still at it when we got to the highway. The only difference was that instead of shouting "I want to go home!" she had turned it into a chant. Yelling the sentence over and over might have tired her out, but repeating it in a singsong rhythm was easy and therefore better suited for the long haul. "I want to go home, I want to go HOME, I want to go home, I want to go HOME."

She was still chanting as we neared the George Washington Bridge. As we slowed down to go through the tollbooth, she said, "I'm going to tell the ticket lady that you're kidnapping me. You're all going to get in trouble!"

Heather, gifted at keeping it light, laughed and said, "Good try, Tasha, but we have E-ZPass."

That night I dreamed I was telling my mother that I needed to move her to a dementia unit of a nursing home. In the dream I felt sick about it, because I dreaded what such a place might be like. She seemed to accept the idea, but I looked away for a second, and when I looked back she was crying, and she said, "There'll never be a world."

In the dream I wasn't sure whether she meant that her world, the world she had a place in, was gone and would never come back, or whether she meant that there'll never be a world humane enough for us to feel fully at home in.

I took her to Elena, her internist, later in the week. I said that something had changed. Elena was from Spain, and was always relaxed and imperturbable, which was normally a wonderful quality. But on this visit Elena may have been too relaxed. After talking to my mother, taking her blood pressure, checking her reflexes, she told me she didn't see the need for any testing.

"Tasha is at an age where we're going to be seeing these changes more often," she said.

But she tried to help, Elena did. She told my mother that she thought she shouldn't be alone anymore, that she should either consider moving or having someone come in to help her. When my mother complained about my taking her car keys away, Elena said that she didn't think she should be driving, but said that if she disagreed, she should get tested. Then she asked my mother why she didn't just take cabs.

"It's my time to go," my mother said.

Elena said, "You know, Tasha, we don't get to choose our time. And we can't keep doing everything we want to do. That happens to everybody. We have to make accommodations."

My mother just looked out the window.

There'll never be a world.

It didn't occur to me until long after this that the fall at Gabe's birthday party might have hurt her badly. She might have suffered a subdural hematoma or some other kind of brain injury.

I don't know whether it would have made any difference if I'd thought of telling Elena about the fall. Would there have been any treatment for a two-week-old hematoma? I've never bothered to look it up, because by the time I thought of it, it was much too late.

I was researching my mother's condition on the internet all the time, as one does.

When a loved one has a dire medical condition and you begin to investigate it on the internet, you can't help thinking that maybe you'll be the person to find the cure, where all the scientists and doctors have failed.

I read an article about coffee and cognition, and tried to make sure she drank coffee every day. It didn't help. My sister read an article about ginkgo biloba. Didn't help. Coenzyme Q10. Alpha-lipoic acid. Vinpocetine. It was remarkable how many surefire cures for dementia the supplement industry had produced.

I read books about caring for the old, the best of which was Atul Gawande's *Being Mortal*.

I'd always liked Gawande's work, ever since I came upon a *New Yorker* essay in which he wrote about his career as a surgeon, exploring the implications of the fact that expertise in any field requires practice, and that you have to be an inexperienced surgeon before you can become an experienced one. He said that when his infant son needed surgery, he made sure it would be done by someone with a lot of experience, but he admitted that if everyone were as knowledgeable a consumer of medical services as he was, novice surgeons would never get the practice they'd need to acquire expertise. I admired his honesty.

Being Mortal is a book about how we treat the old. A book like this is guaranteed to break your heart, because it will make you aware of the very few places where things are done right, which always turn out to be too far away to be of help to you. A nursing home that's affiliated with an elementary school, whose students spend time with the residents every week; a nursing home where each resident is free to decide when to eat, what to eat, when to go to bed, and when to get up. These nursing homes keep residents safe, but they don't equate keeping them safe with controlling them.

Some of these places sounded very much like the classrooms that my mother had run, where the children could learn what they wanted to learn when they wanted to learn it.

You would read about places like this, little utopias in far-off locations, and you would feel even worse about the kind of institution where your parent was likely to end up.

The chapter that did seem to have an immediate use value was the one about gerontologists. Old people's problems aren't the same as young people's problems, Gawande writes, and it's important to have doctors who understand the problems of the old.

As nice as Elena was, she wasn't a specialist in treating the elderly. I began to wonder if a gerontologist might find ways to improve my mother's life.

"I don't need a gerontologist," my mother said.

"Humor me."

"I'm always humoring you. It's like you think you're my parent."

"At a certain age in life, a parent needs their children to take care of them."

"Maybe," my mother said. "But not yet. I'm too young for that."

"You're eighty-six years old."

"Eighty-six is just a kid!"

"Look. I'm going to make an appointment. I'll pick you up at the center, we'll go for a visit, and then we'll have lunch. We'll have a nice lunch."

"You can make all the appointments you want, but I'm not going."

I read about a gerontologist in Hackensack who sounded excellent. People who'd reviewed her on the internet—the adult children of her patients—called her a magician.

On the morning of the appointment, someone from the office called to say that we wouldn't be meeting with the magician but with one of her partners. When I asked if we could reschedule for a day when she'd be available, I was told she had no open slots for the next three months. So I stayed with the magician's assistant.

When you're taking care of an elderly parent, life is filled with what-ifs. What if we had seen the magician? Would things have turned out differently? And it's filled with situations that make what-ifs inevitable, situations in which you have to decide how much you should demand and how little you can settle for. Is this good enough or should I fight for something better? Is the thing I think better really better enough to fight for? Is the thing I think better really better at all? If I fight for the thing that's better and don't get it, will I lose my chance to get the thing that's probably good enough? If she's caught up in the tangles of some bureaucracy and I demand the better thing, will it make the bureaucrats angry at me and will they take it out on her? If I don't demand the better thing, will they think we're pushovers and not give her anything at all? Is there only one right choice in most situations? Or can you almost always get there by another road?

I drove to Teaneck, parked at the seniors' center, and braced myself for the onslaught of adulation. Whenever I walked through the doorway of the center, everyone would look up to see who it was, and they all would seem to be astonished by the good fortune of a visit from such a young man, not a day over sixty. It was like being a weird sort of celebrity, an Elvis of the country of the old.

There was a hitch today, though, in the form of a new member, Gertrude Edelberg, who was the mother of someone I'd been friendly with in elementary school.

"You remember my son Brian," my mother said.

"You're Brian?" she said.

"That's right. It's nice to see you. How's Marty?"

"You're really Brian?"

"Yes. I'm really me."

"What happened to you?"

"I'm sorry?"

"You used to be so slim."

"Well, yes. That was almost fifty years ago."

"I know, but . . . you were so slim. What happened to you?"

"I guess I had too much ice cream."

"Too much ice cream, and too much cake, and too much pie, from the looks of it. Such a shame. I'll tell Marty I saw you . . . if it's really you."

She walked off slowly, shaking her head.

I was Elvis near the end of his life. Fat Elvis.

"To what do I owe this . . ." my mother said, and trailed off, unsure of how the phrase ended. "How come you're here?"

"We have the appointment with the gerontologist."

"With the what?"

"The gerontologist."

"What's a gerontologist?"

"An old people's doctor."

"Why do I need an old people's doctor?"

"Because you're an old people?"

"Forget it. I'll go out to lunch with you if you want, but I'm not going to the doctor."

"I was just going to say the same thing, but different. I'd like to go out to lunch with you, after we go to the doctor."

"Forget it. I'm sorry you drove all the way out here but I'm not going."

I couldn't drag her out, and I didn't want to have a fight with her in front of her people.

"I'll be waiting in the car," I said, "right near the entrance. If you want to join me, that would be good. I'll be there for fifteen minutes. Then I'll go home."

It was a beautiful spring day. I sat in the car with the windows rolled down.

I don't believe in God, but I try to begin every day with a prayer, addressed, I suppose, to life itself. Thank you for giving us this day, which has never been before and will never be again.

I will try my best to love and to make a contribution and to be thankful.

It was my hope that starting the day like this would help me retain a sense of perspective and gratitude even when things were rocky.

I sat in the car, pissed off. I tried to get myself out of my mood by remembering my morning prayer, but it didn't work.

The door of the center opened and my mother appeared, leaning on her cane. I got out and helped her to the car.

"Thank you," I said.

"This is stupid," she said.

The medical office sat above a cramped little parking lot with a lot of girders. I was nervous because I was bringing her somewhere she didn't want to go and I didn't know if it would help at all, and I was nervous, also, about what they might find. Whenever I'm rattled, my driving becomes unreliable. I'm apt to forget the things you need to remember in order to drive a car, such as the requirement that you stop at stop signs. In the parking lot, I was sure I was going to scrape another car. I kept hearing metal on metal.

A few years earlier, I had published a private eye novel under a pen name, and in times of stress I sometimes tried to channel the hero, Nathaniel Singer, a guy who, although Jewish, could do all the things that no Jewish man can actually do. He could change a tire, look under the hood and understand what he was looking at, know whether a revolver was loaded merely from feeling the weight of it in his hand, and get the attention of a waiter in a busy restaurant. In general, he knew how to do things. So now I pretended to be Nathaniel Singer, for whom an ill-designed parking lot wouldn't have posed a challenge. Whether or not it was because I was channeling Singer, I managed to park without messing up anybody's car.

The gerontologist was a woman in her thirties or early forties, with a pleasant air. She got to work quickly, asking my mother if she knew what floor we were on.

"Second floor," my mother said, which was correct.

"Very good," the doctor said. Then she told my mother she was going to give her some tests.

It was what they call a mini mental. My mother was asked to remember three words: *banana, sunrise, chair*. Then she was asked who the president was, and she happily replied that it was Barack Obama. Then she was asked to draw a clock with the hands at ten after ten. She did it carefully and correctly. I was proud of her.

"Very good," the doctor said. "Very, very good."

Maybe I'd been wrong. Maybe there was actually no problem. Maybe her memory lapses were a normal part of the aging process and in no way a cause for concern.

"Now could you repeat those three words for me?" the doctor said.

"What three words?"

"You memorized three words a few minutes ago. You did a very good job with them."

"I don't remember anything about that," my mother said.

"Give it a try."

"If I can't remember them," my mother said, "they couldn't have been too important."

The doctor asked about my mother's medical history, about her diet, about her daily habits. It wasn't clear she was doing anything that any other doctor wouldn't do.

But I'm not sure I would have noticed even if she were. I was too distracted. While she was asking my mother these questions, while she was testing her reflexes, while she was taking her blood pressure, all I could think was *Look at the feet!*

Gawande, in a chapter profiling some perfect gerontologist, right next to the chapter in which he profiled the perfect dementia facility, wrote that he was surprised when, during a session with a new patient, the perfect gerontologist began by looking closely at the patient's feet. "You must always examine the feet," the doctor told Gawande. The doctor went on to tell the story of a "gentleman who seemed dapper and fit, until his feet revealed the truth: he couldn't bend down to reach them, and they turned out not to have been cleaned in weeks, suggesting neglect and real danger."

So I'd expected that this gerontologist would look at my mother's feet. If she had looked at her feet I would have been reassured. If she had looked at her feet I would have felt there was hope. But she didn't. She didn't look at her feet.

Would the magician have looked at her feet?

"So was all that worth it?" my mother said in the elevator.

"I don't think it did any harm," I said. But all I was thinking was, *She didn't look at the feet!*

"I thought I drew that clock very well," my mother said.

It was true. She had.

My sister and Heather and I had been visiting assisted living facilities, and we'd found a place we thought my mother would like. She accompanied us there on a day when they were offering a free lunch, and she admitted it didn't seem so bad, but she wouldn't talk any further with us about moving there. The place—it was called "The Five Star Residence"—offered trial visits, meaning that you could stay there for a week or a month to see how you liked it. But when we talked to her about this, all she'd say was "Not on your life."

At my sister's suggestion, we got together with the rabbi at the Jewish Center to talk about it. Instead of bringing us to his office, he had us sit in the front pew of the large prayer room or sanctuary. Rabbi Zierler was a man who liked to lecture, and I half expected him to climb onto the platform and speak to us from the podium, but instead, he got a chair and sat with us.

Unlike most people who like to lecture, he had intelligent things to say.

"I can understand why you're frustrated with your physical limitations. I can understand why you're so frustrated that you don't even want to think about making a change. But you need to remember that this isn't the entirety of who you are. You're not just the person you are in this moment. You're still all the people you've ever been. You're the young woman who had the courage to leave home at the age of sixteen and live on her own."

"I should have left when I was six."

"You're the young woman who went out into the world and found a job."

"I was the first copy girl at the *Daily Worker*," she said.

"You're the woman who did her part to integrate this town. You're the woman who was an important and beloved educator. You're the woman who brought the open classroom to Teaneck."

"Children's Phone, may I help you please?" she said. "They couldn't believe they were allowed to use a phone in class. But it had an educational purpose."

"You're still everyone you've ever been. Your past still lives within you. And it's important to respect your past and honor your past. And the way to do that is to act in a fashion that's consistent with the way you've acted in the past. You can't do everything that you used to do, but you can continue to be the woman you've always been: the woman who always meets life's challenges in creative and resourceful ways. You have different challenges now. But you can meet those challenges, soulfully and intelligently, and in a way that honors your life and your children's lives. One way to do that is to accept the help they're offering and move into the community they've chosen for you."

My mother was looking around the room.

"I'm not sure you've been listening to me, Tasha," the rabbi said.

"I'm trying to listen, but I can't always understand your vocabulary."

The rabbi kept going. He must have talked without interruption for a quarter of an hour. My mother's body language seemed to be changing. Her resistance seemed to be slackening, either because his arguments were reaching her or because he was tiring her out.

"All your children are asking you to do, Tasha, is to check out the community in Teaneck. Melinda said you can have a trial stay there, for just a week or a month. You've already looked at it with them. You thought it seemed nice, as Melinda told me. All they're asking you to do is give the place a try. Will you agree to that, Tasha? For your own sake, and the sake of your children, and for the sake of your past. Can you do that for us all?"

My mother nodded—I didn't believe this was happening; I didn't believe she could be persuaded to change her mind; it was like the night I went to a bar to watch the Mike Tyson–Buster Douglas fight, thinking I'd only be there for a minute because Tyson had never been defeated and in recent fights nobody'd even taken him past the second round, but this fight went on longer and longer and longer, Douglas kept being surprisingly resourceful, slipping Tyson's punches, working the jab, even starting to seem as if he were gaining the upper hand, it was only around the fifth round that you noticed how much *bigger* than Tyson he was, and finally, it was as if the laws of physics had begun to buckle, Tyson seemed to be getting wobbly, maybe even glassy-eyed, even in the moment when you saw that it was going to happen you still couldn't believe it was happening, but it was true, it was happening, HE'S GONNA FALL—and in a resigned voice, she said, "I guess so."

I leaned back against the pew, exhausted.

"I think it's a really good decision, Tasha," he said. "I think you've made a wise choice."

On the day before we'd agreed to go to the assisted living place, I called her to remind her.

"What?" she said.

"Five Star Residence," I said. "Do you remember? We talked with Rabbi Zierler about it. You agreed to a trial stay there."

"We might have talked with Rabbi Zierler, but I never said I'd go."

"But you did say you'd go. Zierler talked all about, you know, keeping faith with the past, and living in a way that honored all the things you've done in your life."

"I remember he was doing a lot of talking but I couldn't make heads or tails of what he was talking about. He's a very learned man and I like to listen to him talk. But I can't always understand him."

The next morning Heather and I drove out to New Jersey. For some reason I can't recall, Emmett came with us.

My mother got into the car reluctantly. We'd bought her a walker after her fall at Gabriel's birthday party; she hated it, and normally used a cane, but because I thought she might find the day physically taxing, I brought the walker along.

It took me a few minutes to collapse it and fit it into the trunk. I've never been good with spatial relations, or with putting things together, or with taking them apart. When I tried to fold it up, the walker kept baffling me with its complexity. Finally Heather had to do it for me.

"You might need to go to walker rehab," my mother said. "I might have to take your license away."

I hadn't seen her this alert in a long time. Being angry was good for her.

"This is a stupid idea, and I'm not going in," she said. "I'll look at it from the outside, and then we can get some Chinese food."

"It's not exactly Auschwitz, Mom. It's assisted living. It's Five Star."

"Out of how many?" my mother said.

Maybe all she needed, I thought, in order to be at her best, was someone to annoy her, affectionately, for the entire day.

"They probably have ice cream socials there, Mom. You've always been a woman who enjoys a nice ice cream social."

I was trying both to distract her and to lighten her mood.

"What the hell are you talking about?" my mother replied.

"You used to say you didn't want to be around a bunch of old people," I said. "But half the people there will be spring chickens! There'll be eighty-year-olds! Maybe there'll even be somebody as young as seventy-five! Think about it! When you were trying to join the WACS or the WAVES or whatever it was you tried to join, some of these youngsters weren't even born!"

She looked at her watch.

"I'm trying to figure out if it's time for you to shut up yet," she said.

On the way, I succeeded in making her laugh a few times, but I couldn't succeed in softening her mood. She would laugh and then return to her expression of grim oppositionality.

"I'm not going," she kept saying. "I'm not going in there. Take me home instead. Or take me to the city dump. Just dump me with the chicken bones. Or better yet, take me to the cemetery. Save yourself a trip later on."

"Good idea," I said. "All of these are good ideas."

When we got there, she refused to get out of the car.

"I'm very comfortable here, thank you very much," she said.

I went inside and found the person who was supposed to show us her apartment. Her name was Marcia. I told her what was happening, and she accompanied me back to the car. Heather had removed the walker from the trunk and set it outside the passenger door.

"Hey, Tasha," Marcia said.

My mother stared off into the distance, through the front windshield, not deigning to turn toward her or acknowledge that she'd spoken.

"We had an appointment for today. Everyone here is looking forward to meeting you."

Still my mother didn't speak. She was facing straight forward, looking resolutely out the window. She had a lofty expression, as if she were gazing out on vistas far beyond our ken.

"We're looking forward to having you here," Marcia said. "We're looking forward to having you join the community."

Ah, I thought, the community.

A word about the idea of community.

When all this was happening, I was in the middle of a ten-year term as the director of the MFA writing program at Sarah Lawrence. As the director of a writing program, I was forever talking about the idea of community. I would talk about it especially often when I was meeting with prospective students, trying to describe what made our writing program special.

Our community of writers, I would say. Our literary community. Our community of literary voices.

I never actually said "our community of literary voices." I never got that corny. But I came close.

I believed what I was saying, to some extent. When I directed the writing program, I tried to foster an atmosphere in which students were rooting for one another's success, in contrast to those MFA programs famed for their survival-of-the-fittest vibe, where every writer in the program would be happy if every other writer in the program stopped writing or died. It was important to me to try to make our program different. So in that sense the idea of community does mean a lot to me.

But a part of me believes that anybody who talks about community is more likely than not full of shit. Community is rhapsodized about by the same people who like to use the word "folks" and drop their *g*'s, to give their thoughts an air of homespun wisdom. "A lot of folks are lookin' at what's goin' on in the country and askin' if we can't do better. A lot of us older folks are startin' to see that it's the younger folks who are showin' us the way."

And a part of me has more substantial reasons for mistrusting the idea. When we speak of community, we're implicitly talking about a set of social arrangements that includes some people and not others. So then the question becomes: Who's in and who's out? Does the community admit only a certain kind of person? And if the community admits someone who turns out not to be that certain kind of person after all, does the community continue to make them feel welcome, or does it find a way to force them out?

I'd noticed more than once that many students in our writing program could be unfriendly to students or teachers who didn't hold the most up-to-date progressive views, and I'd done little to try to change this. For many of our students, community seemed to mean a group of people who feel the same way about everything. I'd sometimes thought about the beauty of a different idea of community: the idea of a group of people who feel free to disagree with one another and who form attachments through the very act of disagreeing. But I'd never tried to bring it into being.

These were some of the theoretical reasons that made me ambivalent about the idea of community. The nontheoretical reason, the reason I was thinking about any of this as I stood near the car in the parking lot of the Five Star Residence, was that my mother had always been a gadfly, a nonconformist, a disturber of the peace. When she was going through cancer treatments twenty years earlier, she'd shaved her head as soon as the first patch of hair fell out and thereafter had gone around proudly bald, disdaining wigs and scarfs, a rotund sixty-five-year-old woman who suddenly resembled Nikita Khrushchev. At the services she attended on Saturdays, she had defiantly planted herself in the men's side of the synagogue, refusing to move to the women's side until the rabbi asked her if she would do so as a personal favor to him. When she first met the oncologist who'd be overseeing her breast cancer treatments, he had entered the room and said, "Hello, Tasha. I'm Dr. Stevenson," and she'd snapped back, "If you're Dr. Stevenson then I'm Mrs. Morton." Everything I'm talking about came from qualities I loved in her— her lack of vanity or pretension, her belief that everyone is equal and we're all in this together—but I knew that in an assisted living residence, these qualities would get her into trouble. And since she lacked the self-control she used to have (not that she'd ever had much), her nonconformity was apt to get noisy—if not her initial acts of rebellion, then surely her reactions after the staffers predictably tried to shut her acts of rebellion down. I imagined her hurling fistfuls of mashed potatoes at the aides.

"We're really looking forward to having you join our community," Marcia said again.

"Join your own community," my mother said.

"We've reserved a very nice apartment for you."

"Good for you. You should stay there yourself. I hope you have a nice time."

"I don't mind telling you, when I'm just a little bit older, I *am* planning to move here myself. I look forward to taking advantage of the amenities here. Right now I love cooking and cleaning, but when I reach a time when I'd rather have someone else cook my meals and tidy up my apartment, this is where I'm going to be."

"I still love to cook, and I still love to clean."

"You love to clean?" Emmett said.

"I do it all the time. I clean all day."

"Give us a try, Tasha," Marcia said. "We'll take care of you here."

"Go take care of somebody else," my mother said. "Take care of him."

Marcia backed away from the car and gestured for me to join her.

"I'm thinking that our social worker, Valerie, might have more success with your mom. I think the two of them will hit it off."

She went to get Valerie, who came out in a few minutes. At a glance I could tell this wasn't going to work. Just from the way she strode across the parking lot, you could see she was a no-nonsense, take-charge, my-way-or-the-highway person, the kind of person my mother couldn't abide.

"What's this I hear about you not wanting to give us a try?" Valerie said. "From what I'm hearing, you gave your word. You gave your word that you were going to come check us out. Don't tell me you're the kind of person who doesn't keep her word?"

Good way to start. I wished I could disengage for a moment by walking off and smoking a cigarette, but the days when you could do this were long gone, and anyway I hadn't smoked in thirty years. But I walked away nevertheless, imagining how pleasant it would be to smoke right now.

When I turned back, I saw that my mother had gotten out of the car. She was standing at her walker.

Evidently she'd been persuaded to give the place a try. I approached Valerie to find out how she'd done it.

My mother, however, was not heading toward the front door. She was walking in the opposite direction.

"What are you doing, Mom?"

"I'm leaving."

"And where are you going?"

"I'm going home."

"And how do you plan to get there?"

"I'll figure it out. This is Teaneck, right?"

"Yes. This is Teaneck."

"And my house is still in Teaneck?"

This seemed to be a serious question.

"Yes. The house is still in Teaneck."

"Then I can figure out how to get there."

She continued, taking tiny steps, to head for the street.

I joined Heather, Emmett, and Valerie, who were still standing next to the car.

"She tells me she's going home."

"How does she think she'll get there?" Emmett said.

"She says she'll figure it out."

Heather laughed.

"She probably will."

"I don't think there's anything more I can do on this visit," Valerie said. "Mom's not in a listening mood right now."

Mom. I stopped myself from saying, "Is she your mother too?"

"Maybe you can bring her back at a time when she can listen to reason," Valerie said.

That might be a while, I thought.

When Valerie was gone, I said to Heather, "What the hell do we do?"

My mother was making surprising progress. She was on the sidewalk, heading east. She was actually heading in the right direction, except that her home was two miles away.

"Do you want me to talk to her?" Heather said.

"If you don't mind giving it a try."

Heather caught up with my mother while I stayed with Emmett.

"I'm sorry I dragged you into this," I said. "I should have had the sense to leave you at home."

Emmett didn't say anything.

I wondered what he'd make of this experience years later. I wondered what he was making of it now. I'd probably never know.

When the kids were very little, if each of them got a new toy, Gabriel would immediately be all over you, showing off his toy, telling you its name, telling you what superpowers it had and what superpowers it lacked. After he was done, you'd look for Emmett, who'd be nowhere in sight. Finally you'd find him in his room, quietly introducing his new toy to his other toys.

Heather was heading back to us, shaking her head.

"You've got to admire her," she said. "She knows what she wants and she's going to make it happen. And what she wants right now is to go home."

"You think she'd listen to me?" Emmett said.

It would be the act of a cad, I thought, to ask one's ten-year-old son to try to talk sense to one's eighty-six-year-old mother.

"Maybe," I said. "If you don't mind giving it a try."

Emmett trotted off to talk to her.

In difficult situations, Emmett always kept a cool head. Once, for instance, when I was locked in a standoff with the three-year-old Gabe about his desire to rip pages out of a library copy of Perry Anderson's *Arguments Within English Marxism*, the five-year-old Emmett said, "Maybe if you let him sit on your lap and give him a picture book to look at, he'll stop being so angry." I did, and he did. Committed to the battle, I never would have thought of this on my own.

Heather and I watched as Emmett talked with my mother, keeping pace with her, smiling, laughing at something she said. Then he shrugged and started walking back toward us.

"She says I'm a very good grandson, but she won't change her mind," Emmett said.

"Thanks for trying."

"We can't just stand here," Heather said. "We've got to go get her."

"Why?" I said.

"Why? You're seriously asking that?"

"Maybe she's just got to learn her lesson."

"There are a lot of lessons it would be good for her to learn," Heather said. "But I don't think what it's like to get run over is one of them."

My mother was moving slowly but indomitably. As exasperated as I was, I had to admit to myself that there was something beautiful about the sight. Old, frail, disoriented, she nevertheless retained an unbendable intensity of sheer will, trained on the one clear goal of living her own life.

She turned a corner and was lost from sight.

"You're right," I said. "We'd better move."

We all went back to the car. I thought she'd be easy to catch up to. But when we got to the intersection, we didn't see her. I drove down each of the surrounding blocks. She was gone.

"This is getting scary," I said.

"Maybe somebody took her in," Emmett said. "Thinking she was a god in disguise."

He'd recently read a book of Greek myths.

After ten minutes spent driving down each street in the area, I was starting to panic. I think we all were.

"Do you think she could have wandered into somebody's backyard?" I said.

I don't even know why I was asking. Anything was possible, obviously.

"Is that her?" Emmett said.

"I can't see anything."

"Over there," Heather said, pointing.

She was sitting on someone's porch, calmly eating a banana. She must have had it in her purse.

We got out of the car.

"Want a ride?" I said.

"I'm not going back to that hellhole."

"I understand that. I'll just take you home."

"Don't try to force me." She tried to pick up her walker. "I'll hit somebody with this thing."

"Nobody's forcing you. I get it. You want to go home."

"Did you hear that dame? 'We'll take good care of you here.' I bet they take care of you."

"You mean—what? They bump people off?"

"I mean what I mean," she said.

I got a call from Stella, the director of the seniors' center at the synagogue. She was a woman of about fifty who seemed to have wandered out of a B movie from the 1940s—the gravel-voiced sidekick who says the things everyone else is afraid to say. Maybe she was aware of the resemblance. Maybe she even played it up. She'd once put her arm around my mother and said, "We're just a couple of old broads."

She'd always been good to my mother, and my mother had always liked her. You knew where you stood with her.

"I need to talk to you about Tasha," Stella said. "I'm not sure we can keep her on."

"Why? What's happening?"

"Some of the other members are complaining."

I closed my eyes.

"Okay. What are they complaining about?"

"Let me ask you a question," Stella said. "Could you give me an estimate of how often Tasha takes a shower or a bath?"

"I really can't say. Why?"

"There's an odor. You haven't noticed?"

Recently, when I'd picked up my mother to take her out to lunch, I had noticed a sort of baby-powder smell. It wasn't unpleasant, but it was a little strange.

"We're going to have a talk with her tomorrow," Stella said.

"Why don't you let me talk to her first."

"I'm sorry but it's gone beyond that. I'm on the verge of a members' revolt. If you want to come tomorrow, you're welcome to come, but I'm going to talk to her tomorrow either way."

The next day, Heather and I drove to the center. It was summertime, so both of us were free. My sister took the morning off from work and joined us.

When Heather and I arrived, my sister and Stella were already with my mother in Stella's office, waiting for us.

Stella got right down to it.

"We've told Tasha many times that we can't have her coming here like this. It's disrespectful to the staff and it's disrespectful to our other members. And it's disrespectful to herself."

My mother sat there, chin lifted, with a proud expression she sometimes wore, an expression of stoic dignity. With her right hand resting on the top of her cane and her left hand folded over her right, she looked like a Civil War general at the signing ceremony of a great treaty. You could almost see the Mathew Brady photograph.

"We're not asking for much," Stella said. "We're just asking that Tasha practice adequate hygiene, and we're asking her to change her clothes regularly. I don't think you've changed your clothes in weeks, Tasha. You have to change your clothes."

My mother sat, unyielding, not even acknowledging that she was being addressed.

One after another, we all tried to persuade her. Melinda tried, Heather tried, I tried. We all were as reasonable and understanding as we could be, reminding her of how much she loved the center and how much she valued being there. But my mother was like a rock.

I'm sure it was humiliating, but she looked more defiant than humiliated.

As always, I wondered what was going on in her mind.

The question of other minds.

When we know someone well, we can do a creditable job of imagining their concerns. After Holmes and Watson were chatting idly one evening, they fell silent for an hour; Holmes then made a remark that responded to the question Watson had been wondering about at just that moment. Holmes knew Watson's mind so well that he knew precisely where his train of thought had led.

My mother's mind was alien to me now. What was she thinking when she refused even to contemplate the idea of washing regularly and changing her clothes? Was she afraid of taking baths but unwilling to admit it? Had she fallen in the bathtub, and was she afraid that if she told us, we'd put her into a nursing home?

Or was she not thinking anything like this at all? Had she vacated the regions of the mind that engage in anything that you or I would have recognized as thought?

When I was young, she used to divide the laundry into three piles: the lights, the darks, the intermediates. She was bothered when in high school I once washed my T-shirts with my jeans, telling me that my T-shirts would become "tattletale gray." Now the same woman remained obdurately silent when asked to change her clothes.

The transformation hadn't happened overnight, and it hadn't been caused solely by the stroke. Two years before this intervention at the seniors' center, she'd stayed at our house for a week after injuring herself in a fall, and, although she couldn't reach our bathroom, which was on the second floor, she was angry when we bought a commode chair for her, declaring that it was a waste of money ("I'm a Depression baby!") and believing it would be not only thriftier but also just as convenient for her to use the cat litter box.

Today, in Stella's office, we sat like exhausted combatants taking a pause before the next phase of the battle. My mother, actually, was the only one of us who looked as if she had any strength left.

The door was ajar and I caught a glimpse of someone walking past—a silver-haired man in a blue suit. I imagined it was my father, looking for her.

A memory came to mind from long ago: my father arriving home early from work one evening, my mother's expression of delighted surprise.

I imagined him entering the office and finding her as she was now, grimly resistant to our pleas that she consider changing her underwear, almost feral in her refusal to even look at us.

The next time I visited her, I visited her in a mental institution.

I know this isn't a phrase that's used anymore, but with a place like this, only the harsh outmoded phrase will do.

Bergen Pines was a locked-unit psychiatric facility run by the state of New Jersey. When I was young, it was widely known to be a horror show: underfunded and poorly staffed, closer to a prison than to a hospital.

And now that was where my mother was.

Stella had finally relented on her insistence that my mother had to choose between bathing more often or getting banned, but some of the old ladies on the jitney were not so forgiving, and one morning my mother got into a hassle with another old-timer, Faye, which had ended with my mother calling Faye a yekke bitch. (A yekke is a German Jew; my mother hated the yekkes, convinced that they put on airs and looked down their noses at Eastern European Jews like her.) The driver ordered her off the bus. After she refused to leave, he called the cops. And the cops had taken her to Bergen Pines.

Stella called me to tell me what had happened, but all she knew was that the cops had taken her away. I called the police station as soon as we got off. I assumed I'd get shunted from person to person before I could get any information about what had happened or where she was, but it turned out that she was the talk of the Teaneck Police Department that day. The first cop who answered the phone knew all about it.

"Your mother sounds like a real character," he said.

He told me the story and then he said, "You're the writer, right?"

Was I famous? Was I such a famous son of Teaneck that my name was known to the police?

"Your mother kept talking about you. She kept saying you were going to write a book about the Teaneck police force and expose us all."

"I'm already on it," I said.

"You ever written anything I might have read?" he said. "You as good as she says?"

"No," I said. "No to both."

"She told me to read one called *Starting Off in the Morning.*"

My mother was a great promoter of my work, and although she didn't always get the titles right, she always came close.

"She'd actually calmed down by the time I saw her. I wish we could have just got her back home, but they'd already written her up. So we had to take her down to the Pines."

Bergen Pines—well, if you want to see it in your mind's eye, please imagine Dr. Frankenstein's castle, from the old black-and-white movies. A dark, forbidding structure, set back on a hill, on a night riven by lightning and thunderstorms.

This might not be what you'd see if you looked it up on Google Maps, but it's the way I always imagined it before I ever saw it, and it's the way I remember it when I think of it now.

The main entrance of the building was inexplicably locked, and when I pressed the buzzer, no one responded. It took a long time to find another entrance, and then it took a long time to get buzzed in, and a long time to find the unit where she was being held, and a long time to get buzzed in to that. I sat in a gray room with roaches walking over peeling walls. Some of the roaches walked indolently, like stroke victims, and some of them zipped along so quickly you could barely see them. The room smelled strange. You got the sense that there was a row of urinals in the corner, and in your peripheral vision, it seemed to be there, but when you turned to look at it, it was gone.

Finally my mother was brought in.

She was wearing a pink sweatshirt and pink sweatpants, as if she had been swooped up by the cops during a trip to the mall. At least she'd changed her clothes at some point since I'd seen her last. She was clutching a memo pad and a rolled-up tissue. For some reason, she always needed to hold something in at least one of her hands. Often she would hold more objects than she could dexterously handle.

Also, she had a black eye.

"What happened to you?"

"I fell." She said this sheepishly. "I tried to fix an old lady's wheelchair and I fell over."

At least nobody'd been beating her up in here. Life had reached a point at which a thought like this was a consolation.

Standing next to her was a worker of some sort, a pleasant-looking woman in her twenties.

"I'm Lena," she said. "I've been keeping your mother company since she took that fall."

"She's my prison guard," my mother said cheerfully.

"You shouldn't keep saying that," Lena said, smiling. "Someone might think you didn't like me."

"How could I not like you?" my mother said. "You're a living doll."

"You know that and I know that," Lena said, "but does your son the writer know that? He just met me."

"Of course he does," my mother said. "He's an idiot, but he's not a complete idiot."

Even in the castle of horror, my mother had found someone to joke around with.

"She's also the union rep," my mother said. "Your dad would be proud of her."

"Your mother tells me he was a union man," Lena said. "Rough and tumble."

It was true. He was a labor man of the old school. He used to tell us bedtime stories about people like the McNamara brothers, the activists from the Iron Workers union who blew up the *Los Angeles Times* building in 1910. Unfortunately, a janitor was working in the building when the explosion took place, and the furor over his death set the labor movement back by decades. But my father told the story not as a cautionary tale about means and ends—rather, he told it as a story about the labor movement's glory days. "Dynamite, that's the stuff!" he would say as he tucked us in.

"I'll leave you two alone to talk," Lena said. "I'll be right out-side."

"How are you doing?" I said to my mother when we were alone.

"Everyone is an idiot here," she said. "I don't mean her. She's nice. I mean the people I have to do things with. Except for one old man. I think his name is . . . I don't know what his name is. He's the only person you can talk to."

I wondered what this could mean. My mother couldn't keep a conversation going for more than a couple of minutes before cir-cling back around to the beginning. What could it mean for her to say that he was the only person you could talk to?

"What am I doing here?" she said.

"It sounds like you got into an argument with the jitney driver."

"What?"

She was incredulous, as if I'd said she was here because of a skydiving accident.

"I didn't get into a fight with anybody," she said. "I never get into fights. What kind of fight?"

"It's just what I heard."

"When are they going to let me go home?"

"Well, here's the thing," I said. "If they let you go home, they need to know that you're going to be safe there."

"Safe? What are you talking about? Of course I'm safe at home. Where could I be more safe?"

"You're not that safe there anymore. How many times have you fallen and broken a bone?"

"You can fall anywhere. You've never fallen in your life?"

"In your house, falling is easier than in than most places."

"Why is it easy to fall in my house? You think I live on a sail-boat?"

"Living on a sailboat would be safer. It's easy to fall in your house because of all the junk on the floor."

"I've been doing a better job of cleaning up lately."

"I know that, and I also know this is the year the Jets might win the Super Bowl."

"What are you talking about?"

"I know your habits. You get the paper and you just drop it on the floor. You get the mail and you just drop it on the floor."

Why was I getting into the specifics with her? I knew there was no point. You could never argue her into anything, even in the old days; now that she had dementia, if you thought you could argue her into anything you should have been in Bergen Pines yourself.

"I'm going to clean it. I really am. I haven't had time lately, but I'm going to start cleaning it up soon."

"Mom, you just can't live like that anymore. It's too dangerous. If you fell and couldn't get up"—I said, knowing that I sounded like a commercial, but this is just the world we live in: all of us at all times are just a step or two away from being advertisements—"you'd need someone to be there."

"I don't need anyone. I'm perfectly capable."

"Well I guess you'll have to stay here then. Because they're not going to release you if you're still living alone. It's out of my hands."

She didn't have an answer to that.

Sensing an advantage, I decided to repeat myself, to make sure she got it.

"It's really simple. Either you have help at home or you stay here."

"I can't stay here."

"Then you have to have help."

"Okay. Fine. Anything you say."

I knew what that meant, of course. It meant "Stop talking about this so I can do what I want and forget this conversation ever happened."

"I'm going to hold you to it, Mom."

"Fine."

"As a matter of fact . . . lend me your notebook."

She laughed, not knowing where this was going.

I opened her memo pad and wrote: "I, Tasha Morton, do solemnly swear that I will allow someone to live in my house to look after me when I get out of here." And I put a line for her signature.

She read it slowly, very slowly, and then she laughed and pushed it back at me.

"You have to sign it," I said.

"You nut," she said, but she signed it.

I couldn't have gotten her to agree to this just by arguing with her. She was willing to be more yielding because of the element of play.

"Let me get Lena back in here," I said. "We need a witness."

Lena was sitting in the hall, looking at her phone. I explained what we were doing, and she laughed and came back into the room and signed the piece of paper.

"It's a good idea, Tasha," she said. "You could use some help."

"Could *you* come help me?" my mother said. "I wouldn't mind having you around. Even though you're a bit of a yenta."

"I'm a what?" Lena said.

"A yenta. You don't know what a yenta is?"

"I don't!" Lena said. "And I'm not sure I like the sound of it either."

"Can you come live with me?" my mother said. "I'll teach you all the words."

I could picture it, and it was beautiful. Young and energetic and funny and patient, Lena would move into my mother's house and make her last years a pleasure. She'd be even better than the Palestinian cabbie.

"I wish I could," Lena said.

Her pager went off, and she left the room, saying she'd be right back.

"Are you taking me home now?" my mother said.

I had to explain to her that she'd been confined there for a mandatory fourteen-day stay.

"I don't know what I did to get myself into such a murderous situation," she said.

It was time to say goodbye. I stood up and hugged her.

"I love you," I said.

"I always knew that," she said. "But it doesn't help."

When I visited her that weekend, she wanted to talk about how nice my father was.

It was the first time she'd said anything about him in a long time—anything other than talking about how he had a story to tell her in the morning.

"You remember your father? He was a really nice guy."

"I do remember him," I said. "I thought he was a nice guy too."

"You never knew how much he loved you. He never said so but he loved you kids like crazy."

It was true that he never said so, but it wasn't true that I didn't know.

We'd had our own kind of relationship, which was satisfactory to both of us, I think, even if it made no sense to anybody else. You couldn't actually talk to the guy—that, I admit, was a problem. You could talk about history or politics, but you could never talk to him about anything personal. "People say there's not enough communication," he used to say. "I think there's too much communication."

When I read a book I thought he might like, I would never tell him about it or give it to him. Instead, when I'd visit them, I'd leave it in the den or the kitchen, and on my next visit, I'd see it on his night table or near his easy chair. That was our relationship. That was why I didn't need him to tell me how he felt about me.

"He never said it to me either," she said. "He never told me he loved me. Maybe twice he did."

It wasn't hard to believe. I'm sure it was frustrating for her. Sometimes in a restaurant after a drink he would put his pinkie on top of hers and say, "A hearty handclasp." That was the outer limit of his capacity for public displays of affection.

One Saturday morning in high school I got out of soccer practice early and came back to the house when he thought he was alone. He was talking to himself in the shower.

"I'm clean as a whistle," he said.

You're clean as a whistle, I thought. What does the Marxist labor leader say when he thinks he's alone? He says he's clean as a whistle.

Then he said, "Tasha? Tash? I love you, Tasha."

He said it to her only a few times during their thirty-five-year marriage, but when he thought he was alone, he could say it in a voice so strong I could hear it in another part of the house.

When she mentioned his niceness, I wondered what she was leading up to. She seemed to be saying it with a special intent.

"When my parents were coming back from Israel," she said, "I was trying to find a place for them to stay. I was trying to find a rental."

I started to understand where this was going.

"But your father said, 'A rental? Are you crazy? They're staying with us.' And they did. As soon as they got back from Israel, we took them in. I never would have asked. It would have seemed like too much to ask. But your father said, 'Family's family!'"

She let the moral of the story hang in the air. Nice guys take their families in.

Of course I'd often wondered why I wasn't volunteering to take her in.

After her stroke, while she was recuperating, Heather and I had talked about it. Heather said we could make it work. I said I didn't think we could.

After her Helen Hayes adventure, we'd hired a social worker from an eldercare agency to help us think about how to make this phase of her life more comfortable. The social worker, Laura, spent an afternoon with my mother to get to know her, and one of the things she said when she reported back to me was that "Tasha seemed intent on moving in with you or your sister, and I tried to explain to her that this isn't the way things are done anymore."

I was grateful that Laura wasn't guilt-tripping me about this. I could have imagined her interrogating me about precisely *why* I wasn't offering to take my mother in. But at the same time, I didn't think her explanation to my mother made sense. It was comforting to hear her say that this wasn't the way things are done anymore— but why? *Why* wasn't this the way things are done?

Around the same time, I'd started an account on Ancestry.com. I hadn't been able to find out much about my mother's people, since her parents had come over from Poland, and Ancestry.com doesn't follow your family's tracks back to the old country. About my father's family, which had come from Ireland around 1800, I'd learned much more—what many of them had done for a living, where they'd lived and died. They'd been laborers and plumbers;

two had been railroad "yard washers," meaning that they washed the trains; several had worked in a hammock factory. (Hammock factories. Who knew?) One thing I'd noticed was that the mothers all ended up living with their children. In the nineteenth century, in Irish New York, women would marry and raise a family, and after their husbands died, they'd move in with one of their children. Generation after generation, that's just the way it worked.

What had changed since then? Why is it no longer expected, no longer nearly inevitable, that children will take their parents in? I don't know whether adult children in the old days who took in their mothers tended to view it as a pleasure or a pain or simply as a responsibility so unquestionable that it didn't occur to them to have any feelings about it at all. But it was clearly viewed as a normal part of the life cycle (to use a phrase that would have mystified my Hell's Kitchen ancestors and probably made them suspicious of me). When did we decide as a society that it would be better to have our parents spend their last years with people who don't care about them?

These questions were going through my mind constantly, at the same time as I really, really, really didn't want to take her in.

One of the striking things about it all was how little help we could find. How few resources. My sister and Heather and I were knowledgeable medical consumers. My sister had lived through leukemia and a bone marrow transplant; Heather and I had lived through Emmett's four-year tour of medical hell. (He'd been born with a blood disorder, kept alive through monthly blood transfusions, and cured, finally, by a bone marrow transplant when he was four years old.)

Before Emmett was cured, Heather and I had learned everything we could about the causes and treatment of blood diseases. Eventually we knew the name of every top-flight pediatric hematologist in the country: their names, their specialties, their reputations. I remember thinking I knew as much about them as I used to know about Hall of Fame baseball players when I was nine. It got to a point where no one ever recommended a hematologist we hadn't already heard of.

Somehow it was much harder to find solid information that would help us take care of my mother. Are there legal differences between New York and New Jersey that have any bearing on where we should look for a home for her? What does Medicare pay for? What do you need to pay for out of pocket? If you run out of money and you need a kind of service that Medicare won't pay for, how much of the bill will Medicaid pick up? Is it the same in both states? How do you investigate comparative safety rates at old age homes? How do you investigate menschiness rates among the staff? And if we couldn't persuade her to move into an old age home, how could we investigate safety and menschiness rates among home care agencies?

When we were researching Emmett's condition, we felt, in a way, like we were in an orderly world. That he had an undiagnosed blood disorder was terrifying, but we understood the steps we had to take to help him. We knew what tests the doctors would run to try to diagnose him; when, after all these tests, they couldn't come up with an answer, we knew what they would do to treat a blood disorder they couldn't diagnose. He could get blood transfusions for the rest of his life, with other therapies to combat the side effects of years of transfusions, or he could have a bone marrow transplant, a risky procedure but one that offered hope of a cure. None of this was easy but we always knew where we stood.

With my mother, it should have been simpler. Since the end point was never in doubt, the only question should have been how to accompany her there with gentleness and kindness. It shouldn't have been so hard to figure out what she was entitled to and what she wasn't; it shouldn't have been so hard to get a sense of which assisted living institutions were likely to treat her humanely and which were likely to kill her off through repeated small failures of attention. But it was all hard. We got the names of people who could supposedly guide us through the process, but it turned out that they too were working in the dark, trying to pass off their scant contacts and limited knowledge as expertise. This is just how it goes, in a country whose motto might as well be "You're On Your Own."

We'd read about a hospice in New Jersey run by a remarkable man who lived on-site and shared the lives of the dying, and one day I called him in search of advice. He couldn't take my mother in, but he had a list of independent caregivers he said he could vouch for. My sister and I interviewed many people over the next few weeks—my sister did the lion's share—until at last we found Ronnie and Marilyn, two women who worked as a team, Ronnie taking the weekdays, Marilyn the weekends. They talked about how much they loved the people they worked for, how much they loved to cook and clean. We knew they were laying it on thick, but we thought that if they were half as kind and responsible as they claimed to be, Tasha would be in good hands.

My sister and I tried to explain that my mother could be difficult.

"You should have met some of the people I've worked with," Ronnie said. "You should have met Lucy. Believe me, you haven't seen difficult. The crabbier they are, the more I love 'em."

On her second day back from Bergen Pines—her second day with Ronnie—my mother called me late in the evening.

"She isn't feeding me dinner."

"What?"

"She made herself dinner and she didn't give me any. Is this your idea of bringing someone in to take care of me?"

"I find it hard to believe that she made a meal and didn't give you anything."

"You should believe it. You should believe it because it happened."

"Can I talk to her?"

"What?"

"Can I talk to Ronnie?"

"He wants to talk to you."

"Hi," she said. "Mr. Morton?"

"You can call me Brian."

"Hi, Brian."

"How's it going?"

"It's going beautifully. Your mother's great. Everything's terrific. We've been getting along great."

"She says . . . she says you wouldn't give her any dinner."

"Excuse me?"

"She said you made a meal but wouldn't give her anything to eat."

"She said that? No. That's not true at all."

"So . . . she did eat?"

"She hasn't eaten yet."

"It's almost nine o'clock. Are you saying you haven't made dinner yet?"

"I did make dinner. I made a very nice dinner for her."

"I have to say I'm totally confused now. You made dinner for her but she didn't eat?"

"I made steak and potatoes and she said she didn't like the steak. She said it was overcooked."

"So you made her a meal and she refused to eat it?"

"Basically."

"Basically? I'm not sure what you mean by 'basically.'"

"She took one bite and she didn't want any more."

"Did she say she didn't want any more?"

"Yes. She said it was overcooked."

"She said it was overcooked and she didn't want any more, or she just said it was overcooked?"

"What's the difference?"

"There's a difference."

"I don't think there's a difference."

"Well, there *is* a difference."

We were the second- and third-greatest logicians in the world, but I wasn't sure which of us was which.

"She said I don't know how to cook."

"So I'm just trying to get what happened. It sounds like maybe you made her this very nice dinner, and she insulted it, and then you took her dinner away from her? And wouldn't let her eat it even though she may have actually wanted to? Is that what happened?"

"That's pretty much what happened," Ronnie said.

"I can understand it if your feelings were hurt," I said. "But this is who she is. She's an unhappy old lady and she doesn't feel good about not being able to live alone anymore, so she's going to be overly critical sometimes. She's going to take it out on you sometimes."

Why, I wondered, do I need to explain this? She had told me how experienced she was at working with elderly dementia patients. She got so much satisfaction from working with them. We had seen her references. We had called her references, and they'd all had good things to say.

"Is the steak still there? Could you still serve it to her, or did you throw it out?"

Ronnie didn't say anything.

"You threw it out?"

Ronnie didn't say anything.

"Okay," I said. "What I'd like you to do is make her something else. It doesn't have to be a steak. You could make her some eggs, you could make her a sardine sandwich." She liked those loathsome fish. "I'd like her to have something else to eat tonight."

"I can make her some eggs."

"Good. Thank you. And even if she tells you she doesn't like the eggs, don't take them away. Give her time to eat them."

"She should eat them if she doesn't like them? You want me to force her to eat the eggs?"

The crabbier they are, the more I love 'em.

"I don't want you to force her. But she's not in good shape, she's unhappy about a lot of things, and she's going to say some stuff that's hurtful. I'm going to need you to let those roll over you, like water off—"

Like water off a duck? Like water under a bridge? I couldn't remember the expression. I wondered what was wrong with me. Stroke, brain tumor, signs of my own dementia to come.

"The important thing," I said, "is that you need to be kind to her and you need to make sure she's safe and well-fed."

"It sounds like you're asking me to respect somebody who's not respecting me."

"I'm not sure that respect is something you can expect to get when you're working with an eighty-seven-year-old lady with dementia. Do you feel that I respect you?"

"You? Yeah. Sure."

"Good. I think that might be the most you can ask."

"I don't know about that. I've been doing this for a long time. Lucy and I respected each other. We loved each other."

"I think these are important things to talk about, and I want to talk with you more about them. But tonight I'd just like to make sure my mother gets fed. Is it okay if we concentrate on that?"

Afterward I lay on the couch replaying the conversation in my mind.

Was she really used to being treated with respect by the eighty- and ninety-year-olds she worked with? Had she really worked with old people at all? Should we start looking for someone else?

Or could all this somehow be seen as a good thing? We'd worked through a misunderstanding early, instead of starting off on a note of phony comity; maybe everything would be uphill from here.

In the middle of the night, I got a phone call, from a New Jersey number I didn't recognize. It looked official: there were four zeroes at the end.

It was an Officer Fletcher, from the Teaneck Police Department.

"We've got your mom here."

"What happened? Is she okay?"

"She's just fine. She's here in the station with us, eating a Snickers bar. Wait. What is it, Gary? It's a Milky Way. She refused the Snickers. She said she knows her rights."

"What happened?"

"What happened is what happens. She took a stroll down Teaneck Road at one in the morning."

"How'd you find her?"

"A gentleman who almost ran her over gave us a call."

"How did you find my number? She couldn't have had any ID on her?"

"We have your number on file here now, after the Bergen Pines thing. Anyway, the officer who caught the call used to be a student of hers. He comes into the station and says, 'Look who I got here. Mrs. Morton.'"

I drove out to Teaneck. My mother was sitting next to the main desk. Officer Fletcher was at the desk, working on a jumble from a book of brainteasers.

"What are you doing here?" my mother said.

"Just happened to be in the neighborhood."

"But I thought you were in Rockport," she said.

When I was a kid, we used to spend a week or two in Rockport, Massachusetts, every summer. None of us had been there in forty years.

"How's she treating you?" I said to Officer Fletcher.

"She's been giving me a hard time, if you want to know the truth. She has a lot of opinions to share about the Teaneck police."

"There are always kids in the park at night," my mother said. "They should have a rec center, and it should be open all night. They need someplace to go. I'm not talking about all year. I'm talking about the summer."

"It's not a bad idea, actually," Officer Fletcher said.

"Well, Mom. How are you doing?"

"Doing okay," she said. "Want to get something to eat?"

I took her to an all-night diner in Hackensack. She had a cheeseburger and I had two or three cups of coffee.

"So how've you been?" my mother said. "How come you didn't bring the kids with you? I don't see the kids enough."

"It's three in the morning, Mom."

"You're kidding."

"No lie."

"What are you doing out here at three in the morning? You didn't need to come to see me at such a crazy time."

"Well, you know, I was asleep, but then I got up to have a little snack, and I thought, This would be a great time to see my mom."

"You nut."

It was hard to stay exasperated with her because she was always so open to being joked with.

"I'm wondering why you decided to take a walk at one in the morning," I said.

"I woke up and I needed to pee. Then I saw my clock wasn't working and I tried to find that lady to find out what time it was. Then I thought it must be time to wait for the jitney."

When I took her home, I found the front door open.

I walked my mother to her bedroom and went to check on Ronnie. The door to her room was open and the bed was empty. There were little empty vials on the floor. I looked around the house, but she wasn't there.

I called her number and got no answer.

I pulled an easy chair from the living room into the hall between my mother's room and Ronnie's, and was sleeping when Ronnie came in at about five o'clock. She was closing the door of her room.

"Hey," I said.

"Oh, hi," she said. "I didn't want to wake you."

"Where were you?"

"Where was I?"

"Yes. I was wondering."

"I just needed to go out for a little while. I needed to see my sister. She isn't feeling well and I needed to bring her some Advil."

"Are you wondering why I'm here?"

She didn't say anything.

"If I were you, I'd be wondering why I'm here."

I was holding myself back, trying not to explode, but maybe it would have been preferable for Ronnie if I had. I'm sure I sounded tensely on the verge of exploding, and maybe that was worse.

"Why *are* you here?" she said.

"I'm here because the Teaneck police called me at one in the morning to tell me that my mother was wandering around on the street."

"Your mother?"

"Yup. My mother."

"That's weird. You sure *you* didn't let her out?"

"You mean did I drive out here and take her outside, leave her outside, and then go home and wait for the Teaneck police to call me to tell me they found her outside? No, I didn't do that."

She considered this, seeming to agree that it was unlikely.

I wanted to keep going, but I forced myself to stop. None of this was fair. I was a college teacher, with a tenured job. She was working at a job for which we were paying her the going rate—in other words, we were paying her shittily—and she clearly had serious problems. I'd made my point, and it would be ugly to keep making it.

"So, Ronnie," I said, "I think it's time for you to go."

"Beg pardon?"

"I don't want you working here any longer."

"This is really kind of sudden."

"It's kind of sudden because you suddenly left the house and left my mother alone."

"I know I did. But that's not who I am."

That's not who I am.

It's a phrase we hear a lot, from athletes and celebrities and politicians, after a lurid secret has gotten out. It's probably something any of us might want to say, if every gossipy email and every web search and everything we've ever said behind friends' backs were to come to light.

What does it mean, though? Is it totally hypocritical?— something that merely means "Damn, I wish I hadn't gotten caught"? Or does it have a grain of reasonableness? Does it mean "This act was so unrepresentative of me that you should disregard it when assessing my character, much as a kindly teacher will discard the lowest test score when calculating a student's grade"? Something like that?

Would it help us any if we could go a step beyond that and say, "That *is* who I am—I wanted to do it, and I'll probably want to do it again—but it isn't everything I am"? Would it help us if we weren't forever thrusting parts of ourselves into dark corners?

These questions flitted through my mind, but I couldn't think about them now, and I couldn't bring myself to offer Ronnie the forgiveness and understanding that thinking about them might have led me to offer to someone I cared about.

As I sat in the hallway listening to her pack her things, I tried again. A line from Whitman came into my mind: "Whoever walks a furlong without sympathy walks to his own funeral drest in his shroud."

I knew nothing about who Ronnie was or what she'd gone through in life. Trying to call up some sympathy, I reminded myself that she was someone's daughter. I tried to imagine her as a child, in need of protection and care. And I told myself that, whatever the addiction or compulsion that had made her leave the house in the middle of the night, it surely wasn't something she was proud of. In the course of her life it must have given her a great deal of pain.

None of this worked. She'd ducked out on my mother in the middle of the night. I didn't want to think about her problems. I just wanted her gone.

After she left, I sat in the hall outside my mother's room and slept for another hour, until I was awakened by my mother calling out, "Can you help me?"

I went into her room. She had been trying to get up in bed.

"What are you doing here? I thought it was going to be that lady."

I helped her get out of her bed and walk to the bathroom. I was grateful to learn that she still valued her privacy: she let me walk her into the bathroom, and then she leaned against the toilet seat and asked me to leave the room.

I heard the toilet flush and the water running in the sink. So at least she was still washing her hands.

When she got out, she said, "I still can't believe you're here."

She didn't seem to remember the night—leaving the house, the police station, the late-night cheeseburger in the diner. I didn't want to tell her I'd fired Ronnie. She seemed so delighted by my inexplicable appearance that it seemed kinder to make her think I was there simply because on the spur of the moment I'd decided to drive out to New Jersey to see her.

My mother stayed with us for a week while my sister, Heather, and I interviewed a new round of caregivers. I secretly regarded the visit as a sort of test run for me to figure out if I was a nice enough guy to consider taking her in.

Every morning either Heather or I drove my mother across the George Washington Bridge to the seniors' center in Teaneck, and every afternoon one of us picked her up from there. This was only partly because we were nice guys; the other part of it is that we were both working and we didn't have anywhere else to put her. Leaving her alone wouldn't do; when we tried that on her first day with us, she was boiling with anger and a feeling of having been neglected by the time we got home.

She felt neglected even when we were home. She began to get angrier and angrier at my kids. Emmett was eleven and Gabriel was nine; they loved her, but they didn't want to be around her that much. They were deep in their own worlds. Emmett had discovered the pleasures of reading and was never not immersed in a book. "Sometimes I get so lost in a book that I forget I'm me," he once said. Gabe was a serial obsessive, fascinated first by cars and then by pens and now by architecture. When Heather asked him what he wanted to do one lazy Sunday, he asked if they could go into the city to look at the Woolworth Building. At home all he wanted to do was look at picture books of the notable structures of the world. They didn't want to spend that much of their day with an eighty-seven-year-old woman who smelled even funnier than other old people did, who kept trying to grab them and pinch them on the cheeks, and who kept asking them questions and not understanding their answers. She didn't seem to understand that it was natural for them to keep their distance, and soon her un-happiness with them expanded to take in Heather and me. We were encouraging them to ignore her. We were keeping them away from her. We were bad parents.

We were bad parents not just because we were secretly telling our children to neglect her; we were also bad parents because we neglected them. We never made them a proper dinner. (This was true. Unless we ordered takeout, dinner at our house was every man for himself. Emmett calmly made himself a sandwich every night; Gabe whirled around the kitchen, eating peanut butter on a banana as he walked and talked. "I wish aliens would come and do some weird attack on tables so I could eat standing up for the rest of my life.") We let them go outside in their bare feet. (This was also true, and I felt the same way she did about their going barefoot all the time. I suspect that it's ancestral—that Jews don't believe in bare feet, either because we're hypochondriacs and scared of splin-ters or because we retain tribal memories about the importance of being well shod at all times in order to run away from Cossacks. But Heather, a California girl, believed deeply that going around in bare feet was one of the glories of being alive; she thought the practice had health-enhancing properties and was spiritually im-portant as well; and the children had chosen her tradition rather than mine, in the same way that they both said "on accident" instead of "by accident" and insisted on pronouncing the *t* in "often.")

Heather was doing the hard work with Tasha. Heather helped her when she needed help in the bathroom; somehow she even persuaded her to take a bath. And Heather was still telling me that if I wanted to take her in, we could make it work.

But I didn't think we could make it work. It wasn't just that our house was small. It wasn't just that our kids were young. It wasn't just that social expectations had shifted. It was me.

I wanted to keep thinking about it. In the meantime, we'd found another caregiver, named Winnie, who came highly recommended. Of course, Ronnie had come highly recommended too, so we were wary, but we were also hopeful.

Winnie was a skinny, energetic woman in her sixties who'd worked in a hospice until the place closed down, a casualty of bipartisan budget cuts. During her first days with my mother, whenever my mother napped, Winnie set herself to the task of recapturing the house from the elements, attacking decades of neglect with a missionary fervor, vacuuming the carpets and the curtains, scouring the surfaces, opening the windows and letting breezes into the house to chase away the stagnant air. She was like the General Sherman of the Sherwood Avenue campaign.

She wasn't someone my mother could talk with, and she wasn't someone who would try to draw my mother out. I didn't blame her for that, because the effort to talk to my mother never yielded much beyond the few anecdotes preserved in her mind.

I told her what my mother liked to watch on TV. (MSNBC, *Wheel of Fortune*, and, for some reason, *CSI: Miami*. She had a thing for David Caruso.) But whenever I visited, she was sitting blankly in front of Fox News. I wasn't sure it mattered, because my mother couldn't follow what anyone was saying on TV, and after the second time I asked Winnie to let her watch the shows she liked, I dropped it.

I'd also told her what foods Tasha liked, but it turned out that Winnie adhered to a strict idea of what everyone should eat: a diet that was mostly vegan, and that prohibited sugar in any form, but somehow included hot dogs.

During the year or two before her stroke, my mother had finally given up her quest to lose the twenty-five pounds she'd been trying to lose since I was in elementary school, and had thereupon magically lost them. After that, she'd stopped drinking diet soda and started buying cases of Coke. Now when I visited I saw that the Coke was untouched.

"Soda isn't good for you," Winnie said.

"She enjoys Coca-Cola," I said. "There aren't that many things she enjoys, and she doesn't have much time left."

"I'm not going to stand by and let her eat things that aren't good for her. I have a responsibility."

"She's eighty-seven years old. She likes to drink Coke. If it would make her happy to take up smoking, then I'd like her to be able to smoke. In that case, your only responsibility would be to make sure she doesn't burn down the house."

This made Winnie smile, but it was the knowing smile of someone who's come to a decision but remains benignly tolerant of dissent. The Coke remained in the pantry, out of my mother's reach.

It was hard to get a sense of what life with Winnie was like for my mother. Winnie liked to talk about what fast friends they'd become, but I couldn't see any sign of it in my mother's face. Rather, when Winnie talked, my mother would sit there grimacing and rolling her eyes.

We thought this was probably the best we could do. Winnie fell short of anyone's image of the ideal caregiver, unless your idea of an ideal caregiver was someone who enforced a diet of "vegan until six" followed by hot dogs. It was frustrating that we couldn't find someone my mother could connect to. As out of it as she was, my mother still retained her playfulness, and she could still get along well with people who had a sense of humor. She had made friends with Lena at Bergen Pines; she'd made friends with Officer Fletcher.

But Winnie made sure my mother changed her clothes, she fed her, she kept her safe, and she didn't go out to buy drugs in the middle of the night. So although it wasn't what we wished for, we didn't think it made sense to look for someone else.

Writing all this, I'm wondering if it comes off as the grousing of a privileged white guy, ticked off about how hard it is to find good help.

Maybe that's the simple truth of the matter. I can't be sure it isn't. No one can see oneself clearly, and I'm not going to try to cop a plea of *That's not who I am.*

But the way I see it, the problem was never the difficulty of finding good help. The problem was living in a society that only fitfully believes in finding institutional arrangements that will take care of those in need. I don't have the erudition to trace the problem back to its origins—I can't do a polished summary of the tangled history of American individualism—but I think it probably derives in part from the fact that the country that was founded on a myth of classlessness, the myth that any man with enough pluck could strike out on his own and go west and make a good life for himself and his family without anybody's help (a myth that had a grain of truth for certain white men). And I think it derives in part from decades of efforts by Republicans and businesspeople and "entrepreneurs" and "thought leaders" to promote the falsehood that government can only make things worse (Ronald Reagan: "The nine most terrifying words in the English language are 'I'm from the government and I'm here to help'"). And I think all this has left us with a country in which, among many other ills, we have no social arrangements to make it easier for us to care for our parents when they're old, and no arrangements to make sure that those who find a livelihood in caring for the old are well compensated and well educated in the needs of those whom they care for. We're all on our own. We're all on our fucking own.

We arranged to go to a restaurant for my mother's eighty-eighth birthday—my sister's family, my family, a couple of my mother's old friends, and Winnie.

When we got there, Winnie was at one end of the table, eating a garden salad, and my mother was at the other end, shaking with rage.

I sat down next to her and asked her how she was.

"I'll tell you how I am. I can't fucking believe that witch is with us. Why is she with us? Who asked her to this? Was it you?"

At the other end of the table, Heather was making conversation with Winnie, so I wasn't concerned that Winnie would overhear us. Anyway the restaurant was loud. I was leaning over, talking into my mother's ear.

"I don't know if she's a witch or just a bitch," she said.

"Let's just try to enjoy this," I said.

"How can I enjoy this? On a birthday you're supposed to be with people you love. You're not supposed to be with witches and bitches."

"I don't know if you're with witches and bitches. You said she might be a witch *or* a bitch—you didn't say both—and she's only one person, so—"

"Oh, shut up."

When it was time to order dessert, she ordered blueberry pie, bread pudding, a hot fudge sundae, and an ice cream soda.

"That's a lot of dessert," I said.

"It's my birthday, and I can do what I want."

The waiter looked at me inquiringly, and I shrugged.

After the desserts arrived, she didn't actually seem that interested in eating them. It was only after she asked the waiter for a Coke that I understood what was going on. Winnie, at the other end of the table, was watching my mother with what looked like a mixture of annoyance and incredulity, which was exactly the reaction my mother wanted. It was a small revenge for all the soda and all the Milky Ways that Winnie had denied her.

She complained about Winnie every time I took her out to lunch.

"She isn't nice."

"Why? What does she do?"

"She's a bitch."

This wasn't informative. It was impossible to tell whether she was complaining because she'd complain about anyone who lived with her or whether there was really something troubling going on. My mother's memory was so poor that even if Winnie were doing malevolent things when they were alone, she wouldn't be able to tell me about them.

With Winnie in the house, at least I knew that if my mother were to fall again, she wouldn't lie on the floor for a day and a night, unable to get to the phone, but I didn't know Winnie enough to trust her, and when it came down to it, I didn't like her. I could see that her impulses were harsh, almost punitive. Lately she'd stopped letting my mother drink the seltzer I bought, saying that water was better both for digestion and for mood.

"The bubbles make you angry in your blood," she explained. "Once you get used to only water, it calms you all the way down."

During Thanksgiving week we brought my mother to our house for a few days. I had hoped some time with us would lift her spirits, but she had a sadness that was beyond anyone's reach. When we sat down to Thanksgiving dinner she said, "Dick used to love to carve the turkey," and started to cry.

My father didn't love to carve the turkey. Though it seems like an odd word for a flinty Irishman, my father was kind of a klutz. In that respect he was an honorary Jew. She was the one who carved. But she was crying anyway.

Inflected by her dementia, her sadness went off in weird directions. When Heather took the kids out to play in the snow and the three of them were gone for an hour, my mother became certain that Heather was planning to leave me.

"So are you going to stay here?" she said. "Are we all having dinner?"

"Yes. Of course."

She let out a deep sigh.

"It's sad that they have to see this," she said. "The breakup of two families."

I didn't know, and will never know, who the second family was.

When, on Saturday afternoon, I told her that I was taking her back to her house in the morning, and that she'd still be living with Winnie, she cried.

"How can you do this?" she said.

That evening I drove to an electronics store and bought a small recording device, which looked like an ordinary flash drive. When I took my mother back to her house, I put it in the den, where she and Winnie spent most of their time. The place was no longer a monument to my mother's hoarding skills, but it was still so cluttered with tchotchkes that concealing the flash drive wasn't difficult. I retrieved it a week later and listened to it when I got back home.

Early in the recording, a TV show was on, and in a scene set in an office where the phone kept ringing, my mother, thinking that her landline was ringing, kept picking up the receiver and saying, "Hello?"

Every time she did so, Winnie would say, "Shut your mouth!"

Later, Winnie was talking on the phone, and my mother, hearing her words but evidently not seeing the phone in her hand, said, "Excuse me?"

I heard Winnie say, "Hold on a second," to whoever she was talking to. Then she said, "Shut up. Just be quiet and shut your mouth. Nobody wants to hear from you."

When she ended her conversation, she said, "Why don't you shut up when I tell you to shut up? No one's talking to you!"

"Someone *was* talking to me," my mother said.

"Who's going to talk to you? Nobody wants to talk to you!"

"That's not true," my mother said. "I get phone calls."

"You only get phone calls from your children, and that's because they have to call! Nobody else calls you! Nobody calls you because you're so ugly! Nobody likes you! You have an ugly face and you have an ugly soul!"

"Bitch," my mother said.

"You have an ugly face and you have an ugly soul and you have an ugly mouth. You have a dirty, dirty mouth."

"I do not have a dirty mouth!"

"You have a mouth so dirty I should wash it out with lye soap! You have a mouth so dirty I should wash it out with ammonia!"

"Don't you dare!"

"I could wash your mouth out so it wasn't so dirty but there's nothing I could do to make your face less ugly! You're so ugly! You're ugly and you have no friends! And when you die no one is going to come to your funeral! Everyone will be happy when you die! If they come to your funeral it will only be because they're all so happy, and they'll want to make sure you're dead! When they lower your coffin into the ground, people will be dancing! Yes, that's true!"

"Nobody will be dancing! That's not true!"

"They will! They'll be dancing! And I'll be dancing with them! I won't even want to go to your funeral, but I'll go anyway, to make sure you're dead and to dance about it! In other people's funerals everybody throws a little dirt on the grave, but at your funeral they'll be throwing—what's that called—they'll be throwing confetti!"

My mother didn't say anything, but I could hear her whimpering.

Later there was another exchange. Winnie was on the phone. She stopped her conversation to say to my mother: "What are you doing?"

"I'm going to the bathroom."

"No you are *not*! I'm on the phone right now and I can't help you. Don't be rude!"

"I'm not being rude. I have to go. I can go on my own."

"No you cannot go on your own. Just stay there. Just stay there and piss in your pants like you always do. Just stay there and piss in your diaper like a little baby."

When I was listening to all this, along with all the other thoughts, I found myself thinking, At least she doesn't beat her. At least she isn't torturing her physically.

In this, the cruelest of the capitalist democracies, if you listen to a recording of your mother with her caregiver and you find that although the caregiver has been verbally abusing her, she hasn't been physically abusing her, you have good reason to feel relieved.

Heather and I went to the house the next day and I asked Winnie if we could speak together alone.

I told her about the recording device and said we wouldn't continue to be employing her. I told her that we'd give her two weeks' pay.

"What are you talking about? I've been nothing but good to Tasha."

"I know that's not true. I know you haven't been good to her."

"How? How have I not been good to her? Tell me one thing."

I think there was a part of me that was waiting for this. A part of me that wanted to do this.

"Well," I said, "if you really need to hear it."

I played her the part about my mother being so ugly that people were going to be dancing at her funeral.

As Winnie listened, she looked like someone might look while listening to a recording not of oneself, but of one's child. She looked the way you might look if you were confronted with proof that your child has done something far worse than you'd imagined possible. She looked genuinely disappointed and surprised.

"I forgot myself that time," she said quietly.

After that, to her credit, she didn't argue, and she didn't ask any more questions.

Well, she did ask one.

"Can I say goodbye to Tasha?"

When she said goodbye to her, my mother didn't understand that she was saying goodbye for good.

I stood in the doorway of the den, watching, and the crazy thing about it was that there was obvious warmth in Winnie's voice. She was sorry to be saying goodbye.

Heather stayed with my mother while I drove Winnie to the bus stop. She had a suitcase with her. I said I'd send her the rest of her stuff.

She was crying in the car and talking about my mother in a disconnected way. She wasn't exactly talking to me, but she wasn't exactly talking only to herself.

"Tasha knows what blouse matches her pants. I don't choose her clothes. I just help her put them on."

"Nobody's nicer than Tasha when she gets over being angry."

"It's a hard job. Sometimes I don't even get any sleep. The night before last, I was up all night. I let her keep those chocolate candies your sister bought, and she was eating those candies all night. I couldn't sleep, because I could hear the bag crackling in there all night."

"She's stubborn, so whatever she wants to do, unless it's dangerous, you just have to let her have her way. She says that's just how she was born."

We waited in the car until the bus came. Then Winnie got out, dragging her suitcase. I helped her with it as she stepped up onto the bus, and then the doors closed.

We took my mother back to our house and she stayed with us while we tried to figure out what to do.

On a Saturday morning I drove her to the Jewish Center, and then, instead of going home, I went to the Hackensack River. I was near the spot where I used to go in high school when I wanted to be alone and mull things over. They'd closed off an old road and you couldn't get there anymore. I was also near the spot where the river had forced its way into my mother's car, ending her life as an independent woman.

I sat on a long flat rock by the river and tried to think.

I'd once infuriated a girlfriend by innocently telling her one of my dreams. I'd dreamed that I was in my apartment during a snowstorm, and I discovered that the apartment had double-pane windows, and not the slightest hint of the storm could make its way in. I told her how happy this had made me in the dream. The two of us were in a restaurant; she shot up out of her chair and said, "You and your double windows! That about sums you up!" Eventually she sat back down, but we both knew it was over.

Double windows, deadbolts, padlocks, fences, moats—these were my friends. When I was growing up, my mother would enter the room without knocking—my bedroom, my sister's—and she resented the suggestion that she *should* knock. She didn't so much resent it as laugh it off. "Knock? I'm your mother!" When I was in high school, as we've seen, she was famous for making panic-stricken phone calls if I was reckless enough to go to a friend's house for a game of after-school Ping-Pong without letting her know. When my sister bought a copy of Kahlil Gibran's *The Prophet*, my mother picked it up and came upon the part about children—"though they are with you yet they belong not to you"—and tossed it on the couch and said, "That's ridiculous. Who else do they belong to?"

Even when I was out of college—living in New York and working—none of this really changed. In my late twenties I spent the night with someone and came home to twenty-seven increasingly distressed phone messages. I didn't need to count. It was in the days of answering machines, and the number was lit up in red.

Learning to hold her at a little distance had been a lifelong effort. It wasn't until I read a book about the family therapist Murray Bowen's theories of "individuation" that I found my way. One of the ideas I took from it is that when you make more room for yourself, it upsets the family system, and other family members will fight you, but if you calmly persist you'll be able to breathe more freely, and they, as much as they fought you in the beginning, will benefit in the end from what you've done. They too will breathe a freer air. Another is that you can do this without breaking all ties; you can do it while keeping your connection; you can do it with love. In my late twenties, after it became clear to my mother that I wasn't going to be available to her in the ways I always had, she was angry and hurt, but within a few months, our relationship had gotten easier and better.

The question I needed to ask myself now was whether I was reluctant to take her in only because I was trapped in the past, still so committed to warding her off that I was failing to come to terms with my responsibilities.

After all, the woman was in need, and I, as the only one of her children who hadn't undergone a bone marrow transplant, was clearly the person who had to help her.

Life gives us a limited number of chances to be the people we want to be.

We had a small house, but we could move. We could sell her place and use the money to buy a house that had room for her and an aide.

I tried to imagine what that would be like, for her and for us.

A week earlier, a friend of Gabe's had come over, and Gabe, out of pure goodness, took him into the living room, where my mother was sitting, to introduce him. She didn't want to let them go.

"Where do you think you're going? It's freezing out there."

Gabe held up his Frisbee.

"Not in this weather. You can play right here."

"We'll be okay, Mima," Gabriel said. He kissed her on the cheek, and his friend waved goodbye and said it was good to meet her.

"Your children aren't nice to me," she said to me after they'd gone out. "Do you tell them not to be nice to me? Do you tell them I don't count?"

A few days before that, just after Heather and I had taken her in, the two of us celebrated our anniversary. We'd made a dinner reservation weeks in advance, and one of the kids' old babysitters, a kind and sensitive young woman they called Amez, was going to look after my mother.

"I'll come with you," my mother said. "It'll be fun."

"It's our anniversary," I said.

"You already told me that. So what? You wouldn't *be* here if not for me."

"I'm sorry, Mom. We'll take you out to dinner on the weekend."

"You didn't think of taking me? You didn't even think of it?"

When Heather and I left the house, my mother wouldn't look at us.

The wind off the river was chilly. I got up and walked toward the car.

A care facility would be better. She'd have companionship; she'd have activities; she wouldn't be reliant on a single aide. We wouldn't be disappointing her every day.

You can be good to her without putting her at the center of your life.

This, at any rate, was what I told myself.

We made arrangements for Tasha to move into the dementia unit of an assisted living residence called Van Buren Manor. She didn't want to, but there wasn't much strength in her refusals anymore.

When we toured the place with her, it was a gingerly endeavor, as I kept trying to get her to see the good side of living there, and kept trying to get myself to see it too. The woman who showed us around was joking with her, which seemed like a good sign.

A friend of my sister's put us in touch with a capable and patient young woman named Dee, who was able to stay with Tasha and serve as her caregiver for two weeks while we made the arrangements to move her to Van Buren.

On the day Tasha was slated to move in, Heather and I came to get her. She was still asleep at noon. Melinda and Heather and I had already moved furniture and clothing and other necessities into her room at Van Buren, so all we needed to do now was drive her there.

Heather was on one side of her and I was on the other as she, leaning on her walker, went slowly down the hall that led to the front door of her house.

You could almost say that over the last thirty years her relationship with her house had been the most important relationship in her life. She'd loved it and felt trapped by it, she'd anguished over it, she'd mistreated it and it had mistreated her.

When she reached the front door, she turned around and looked back.

"So I won't live here anymore?" she said.

Van Buren was in a quiet town in New Jersey, across the street from a long calm park. It had a pleasant garden and the rooms were nice—clean, modern, private, not too small, each with its own bathroom and kitchenette.

She'd be living in the "Free Spirits" wing, a locked unit on the second floor. The Free Spirits wing: it sounded like something out of a Jerry Lewis movie, where the inmates cavort across the lawn while attendants chase after them with butterfly nets.

After we arrived, one of the people who managed the place accompanied us to the unit and left us in the dining room, where the residents, having just finished eating lunch, were being led by aides back to their rooms or to a nearby "activities room" where a large TV screen was mounted on the wall. No one seemed to be responsible for welcoming my mother; there didn't seem to be any protocol for smoothing our goodbye. It was like we were expected just to dump her here and go.

It's curious how few institutions seem to understand the importance of the first day.

Norman Mailer, writing about Frazier and Ali: "The first fifteen seconds of a fight can *be* the fight. It is equivalent to the first kiss in a love affair." And the first fifteen minutes in a place can *be* the place. My mother sat unregarded in a room that had been vacated by everyone who lived or worked there, as Heather and I sat beside her, wondering what was supposed to come next.

Finally Heather got up and found the kitchen and brought my mother a tuna sandwich.

It happened to be my father's birthday. The last birthday he'd lived through had been thirty-one years earlier. That afternoon I'd bought him a book I thought he might like, *Communists in Harlem During the Depression*. It was during a bad time for books in New York, a moment when the little independent bookstores were dying and the superstores had not yet been born. So in order to get it, I looked up the author, Mark Naison, in the phone book, and called him, and took the subway into deepest Brooklyn to his home. On the way back I got on the wrong train, an M train, which takes you into lower Manhattan and turns north only to curve back and return to Brooklyn, so I was late for the dinner.

I can't remember anything about that last birthday dinner, only that I was late getting there.

Now, in the Free Spirits wing, my mother didn't know it was my father's birthday, and I didn't mention it. After she'd finished picking at her sandwich, we wheeled her to her room—they'd given her a wheelchair when we arrived, and she seemed content to remain in it—and I sat with her while Heather put family photographs on the wall. Pictures of my father and Tasha's father (the elusive Chaim), pictures of Melinda and me and our children. Pictures of my mother with each of us in happier times.

She looked at the pictures for a long time.

"Is my mother still alive?" she said.

Later she pointed to one of the photographs of my father.

"Do you know who that is?" she said to Heather.

"Of course. That's Dick," Heather said. "That's your man."

"He said he had a funny story to tell me. But he was tired. He was going to tell me in the morning."

Sometimes I think that parts of our souls are sheared off and left behind in the places that have caused us pain. Whenever I drove near the spot in Hackensack where my mother had gotten caught in the flood, I had the feeling that a part of her was still trapped there. I had had that feeling when I'd sat near there a few weeks earlier. And a part of her had remained in their bedroom, never having moved on from the moment when she touched his arm.

We took her out to the activities room. Most of the old people were sitting in front of the TV screen that dominated the space, watching an episode of *Meerkat Manor*. Others were staring at nothing. The aides were all looking at their phones.

Heather and I stayed until dinnertime. We had thought it would be the best time for a transition—there was an early dinner, then a movie, then bed—but in the dining room, as the aides helped the residents to their tables, one of the residents, a woman, began to shout about being held prisoner there, and another woman screamed at her to shut up, and none of the aides tried to calm them down. I hoped we hadn't delivered her to a house of horrors.

"How long will I be here?" she said.

"I'm not sure," I said, truthfully.

"Are you staying here too?"

Evidently she thought this was a hotel.

"We're going back home. But we'll be back to see you soon."

When we left it was like saying goodbye to your child on the first day of kindergarten, except worse.

The best thing about the weeks that followed was seeing how she loved her morning aide.

Is it true that there are some people who are so good that their goodness is instantly, radiantly clear? Who you don't have to look at for more than five seconds in order to be sure? I distrust the idea, because the world is full of con artists and because I've more than once been wrong. But Cece was one of those people who made you think it was true. You could see it in her face; you could see it in her gentleness; you could see it in the rapport she and my mother had from the first.

During one of my visits my mother said, "Some of my colleagues are very good here. Cece would be a good teacher. I'm going to try to help her get a teaching job. Maybe we can be coteachers."

The night aides were harder to get a fix on. The first one seemed so harsh and barking that we immediately asked to have someone else take over her nighttime care. Her new aide, Bella, spoke in a voice barely louder than a whisper and was forever touching my mother's shoulder and asking if there was anything she could do for her, but one of their encounters left a bruise on my mother's cheek.

Bella said that when she was trying to help my mother off her bed, my mother had grabbed the telephone from the nightstand

and thrown it at her. When she put up her hands to protect herself, the phone rebounded and hit my mother in the face.

When I asked my mother what had happened, she said Bella had hit her, or maybe it was someone else.

I didn't know what to believe, and I didn't know what to do. Demand that my mother change aides again? Move her somewhere else? Try to find a caregiver more humane than Winnie or Ronnie and find another house for us all to live in?

Her room was uncluttered, so I couldn't use the recorder I'd used in her house. It had a red light that flashed on and off when it was working, which made it difficult to conceal. There were no calendars from the 1980s to bury it under, no broken items from the SkyMall catalog to hide it behind. But without a recorder, how could I tell what was going on?

You could hope that the fact that there were many aides and many residents, rather than one aide living in her house with her, would lessen the chances that anyone would be abusive, but if you were in the mood to imagine the worst, you could easily imagine that this was the kind of nursing home you used to read about during the muckraking days of the *Village Voice*, one of those places that fostered a culture of collective cruelty, with all of the aides taking part in it so routinely as to forget they were doing anything wrong.

I visited another place, a Jewish home that had a great reputation—it's like a country club, a social worker had told me—but there was no way of knowing if it would be any better. The woman who ran it talked a good game—she talked about all the activities the residents were offered, all the thought that had gone into designing their environment—but when I visited the main room it was the same old bullshit, with the residents nodding out and the aides looking at their phones. You couldn't blame the aides: they were undertrained, underpaid, unorganized by any union, without rights in the workplace or much of a stake in the residents' well-being. This was just the way things were, in the land of no mercy.

We decided to keep her where she was. Although I couldn't conceal a recording device in the room, I found a workaround: I bought a cheap computer, figured out how to control it remotely, and left it on in her room. From my computer at home I could turn on the voice function in Google Hangouts and listen without anyone's knowing.

I could listen, but I couldn't see anything. And it was hard to be sure what I was hearing.

"That hurts."

"We're just going to get it over with." This was her nighttime aide, Bella. "It doesn't hurt that bad."

"How do *you* know?"

"Just another minute."

"Ow. You're hurting me. I hate you."

"Well, I love you, Tasha."

"You don't even know me. If you loved me you wouldn't be hurting me."

"I do know you, and I love you because God tells me to love everyone."

"Tell him to go fuck himself."

Silence from the aide.

"You're hurting me. I wish you'd never been born, you bitch."

"Why do you have to use that kind of language?"

"I have to because you're a bitch."

Was Bella treating her roughly? Or was my mother just angry and humiliated because she'd been reduced to wearing a diaper and having other people clean her? I recorded the conversations and listened to them repeatedly—no researcher studied the Zapruder tapes more closely than I listened to my mother's conversations with Bella—but I couldn't tell.

I visited her every other week. Melinda would see her on one weekend and I'd see her on the next. I would have thought this schedule would make my mother angry, but when we told her the arrangement, she got teary-eyed with happiness, as if she was grateful that we'd given her enough thought to make any arrangement at all.

When Heather and I arrived one afternoon, she began shaking when she saw us. She looked delighted but also deeply worried.

"How did you get here?"

"We got here the same way we always get here. We drove."

"How did you drive? Everything's going crazy."

She gestured toward the TV screen on the wall. The disaster movie *2012* was playing. John Cusack was driving through a collapsing Los Angeles. Buildings were falling all around him, while his car remained miraculously unscathed.

"That's a movie, Mom. That's not the news."

"You made it through all that to visit me?"

We wheeled her to a quiet lounge, and once we got there, Heather laid out a row of chocolates. For my mother, it was always the high point of the visit. We'd put out some Hershey's Kisses or some Fun Size Milky Ways, and she would pick one up and slowly, carefully, attentively peel off the wrapping. When she was done, she always looked proud.

When we sat with her in the lounge, other residents would come up and talk to us.

There was Al, who was nostalgic for a life at sea. He always wore a nautical captain's hat and a blue blazer with shiny golden buttons. One day when Heather was wheeling my mother to her room and I was walking behind them, Captain Al caught up with me and urgently took my arm.

"I never slept with her," he said.

There was the man who patiently, lucidly, convincingly explained to you that his family had left him here by mistake and were coming to get him. He explained this to us every time we were there.

There was the woman who said to Heather, "Will you remember me? Will you remember me when I was young?"

When we were sitting with my mother in the lounge one afternoon, she looked at the other residents and shook her head incredulously.

"Some of these people actually live here," she said.

After we moved her to Van Buren, she took just one more trip into the outside world. I'd published a book, and when a bookstore in Teaneck asked me to read there, I said yes, because it would be easy to take her there and because I wanted her to attend one of my readings one last time.

After we'd been driving for a while, she said, "This is Teaneck?"

I said yes, and she looked out the window as we passed local landmarks she'd passed hundreds or thousands of times.

"It's like a foreign country," she said.

At the bookstore the audience was small, consisting almost entirely of people who had known my mother in town. I read for just a few minutes, not wanting to tax anyone's patience, and then we had a question-and-answer period. Because it was a hometown gathering, I asked them all to introduce themselves. Almost everyone talked about when they'd met Tasha or when they'd met me. When it was my mother's turn, she took a moment to puzzle out her relationship with me, and then said proudly, "I'm the daughter of the author."

My sister and Heather and I started clearing out my mother's house. During one trip, under a mound of old clothing that my mother had been planning to take to Goodwill any day now for thirty years, we found a folder filled with letters of appreciation from her students' parents. The most touching were the ones she'd received at the beginning of her career, when she taught classes for children who were classified, in the argot of the time, as "brain damaged"—letter after letter from parents whose children had been considered unteachable until my mother worked with them. A letter to her principal in 1963 said, "She not only has helped my son but she has taught me to know and understand him better. I've spent a short time each day in her class and believe me I've seen small miracles come about month after month, children that had no interest in anything suddenly begging for more and more work." In a letter to her superintendent of schools the following year, another parent wrote, "If this were a story rather than a letter it might be entitled 'A Miracle in Teaneck.' In just four months Jack has progressed so much and has in many ways become a very different child . . . We have made a few visits to the school and watched the way she treats children who have similar problems. Every one of them is at a different learning level, with a different personality and with similar but different problems. To her each of them is very special. How one person can do so much with so

much love and understanding and yet with so firm a hand is un-
believable."

I wished we'd found these letters years ago, when we could have
shared the pleasure she would have gotten from seeing them again.

On another trip, cleaning out her bedroom, I found a black-
and-white composition book, the kind that kids use for school.
She'd used it as a diary. She'd started it in 1990, when she'd been on
her own, retired, widowed, for more than five years, and she kept
it up intermittently, often writing nothing for one or two years at
a time, until 2002.

I wasn't prepared for what I read.

She'd never been reluctant to tell me how unhappy she was,
but even so, reading about it in detail took me aback—reading, for
example, two different entries about how hard it was just to get
herself out of bed in the morning, written ten years apart.

Also surprising was how distant she found me. I knew, of
course, that she always wanted more from me, but nevertheless
I thought I gave her a lot—a lot of time, energy, attention. That
wasn't the way she saw it, at all.

Most startling of all were the notes of introspection all through
the diary. In one entry, she wondered whether she'd been deceiving
herself in believing that her depression was caused by my father's
death. Maybe, she said, it had always been there, and he'd pro-
vided more stability than she'd realized. In another she wondered
whether she was asking too much of Melinda and me. Maybe, she
said, "I could do more to help myself feel better and not rely on
them so much."

She'd never shared such thoughts with me. I wished she had. Maybe, I thought, I could have helped her. I don't mean the kind of help she'd always claimed to want—sitting in her den with her, going over every twenty-year-old newspaper and every swizzle stick—but the kind of help I might have given, or might have steered her toward, if she'd admitted she might benefit from having people to talk to.

It would have been simpler, emotionally simpler, if I'd found the diary only after she was dead. It was strange to discover more about her inner world when she was still alive but no longer able to explore it. This terrain, in which she meditated on her life and questioned her own choices, was not a place she'd ever be able to get back to.

What had been frustrating, when she was younger, was that I knew she could do better. I knew she could grow. And now it was heartbreaking to find out how much she'd wanted to grow.

Four or five years after my father died, she'd spent a week in Chautauqua, the little utopia of lectures and learning in Upstate New York, staying with friends who had a place there. She'd gone to all the lectures and performances, and she'd been in heaven; when she called me from there one evening, I heard an excitement in her voice that I hadn't heard in years. She had to rush off the phone to get to another event, which was something like a first for her—she never was the one to end the phone call.

A few years after that, she attended a conference in New York on John Dewey and progressive education, encountering people she hadn't seen in years and people she knew about only from reading their books, educators like Theodore Sizer and Deborah Meier. Her interest in staying on the board of education had been flagging during the previous months, because she was tired of being in a minority of one, but when she called me after the first day of the conference, she said she'd decided to run for another term. "I've still got some fighting to do." When we were getting off the phone, she said she knew she wouldn't be able to get any sleep that night, because she was so excited about everything she was going to learn the next day.

I used to keep hoping she'd find something that would help her sustain that love of learning, turn it into a source of perpetual refreshment.

In her diary, every few years, there are entries that show that she was capable at least of finding momentary joys. She talked about how happy she was when she bought her first computer and learned to use email; she talked with pleasure about a new car. But the depression was always there, only faintly battled against, only faintly examined. I don't know if asking for help would have made anything much better, but it might have.

I don't know why she was never able to rebound after my father died. As she acknowledged, if only in the diary, she was suffering from something more than just the grief of having lost him, but she never came close to understanding what it was, or how she could fight it or cope with it or work with it.

In Stendhal's notebooks, which I looked at long ago, when I was in college, there appears a phrase that has stayed in my mind. "By another road." I can't remember what he meant by it, but over the years, as it's kept coming back to me, it's taken on a particular meaning. I sometimes think it sums up everything we need to know about psychic health. By another road. If the road you'd hoped to travel is closed off to you, you can almost always find another.

When she was young, my mother seemed to live by this idea. When she was mistreated by her parents, she left home. When my father wouldn't marry her, she went to Israel and plunged into life on a kibbutz. When he wasn't talking to her, she packed the children off to Pittsburgh and demanded that he open up.

But by the time she was older, she seemed to have forgotten the idea, or maybe she'd simply lost the strength to live by it.

Maybe it's unreasonable of me, even unkind, to be disappointed that she didn't continue living in this way. Maybe it's just too much to hope for. People grow tired. She grew tired.

But still. I wish she'd gotten help. I wish she'd escaped from that house. I wish she'd let us enroll her in the driver's rehab class. I wish she'd learned to take a damn cab.

I've been going back and forth about whether to include any passages from her diary. Since she's not here to give her permission, it doesn't feel quite right. But since I've already committed myself to writing all these pages about her—also without her permission—I think that including some of her words would be better than not including them, to give her a chance, if only for a few paragraphs, to speak in her own voice.

So here are a few of the entries from her notebook, on the cover of which she'd written, *Thoughts of Tasha Morton (not for anyone else). Keep Out.* I'll leave the spelling and punctuation as they are.

July 10, 1990: "I am starting a diary. Brian suggested it as a memory enhancer. I also hope that there may be a therapeutic value to it. Maybe I'll finally find out something about myself."

July 17, 1991: "So much for a diary. A whole year has passed. I am the worst procrastinator there ever was. I found this as I was going through the usual of trying to clear up my excess paper and found this so I feel compelled to write again. But I am keeping away from my personal thoughts-feelings. What's the point if I can't be open with myself."

August 27, 1991: "Why is my son so hard on me? I walk on eggs when I am with him or even talk to him. I don't have the courage to get angry at him. There is too much of his father in him and who knows how long he could go without talking to him.

Am I ridiculously sensitive or what. Melinda has become a namby-pamby. At times like this I have to give myself reasons to exist. What will happen if I really become a burden to my children. I feel like an infant who wants to run away or do something to make her children pay attention. It's back to when I was a kid and day-dreaming my own death. And feeling I would be the only one to cry. I think I am becoming a manic-depressive. Maybe I should be taking lithium. Shit. I'm going to bed."

August 28, 1991: "I feel somewhat better but I still think I'm somewhat nuts, too. Was I always like this. I don't think so, but maybe I'm fooling myself and my ups & downs didn't start with Dick's death. Maybe in his way he was able to give me stability."

November 13, 1993: "I am writing during a board meeting. I am bored with the budget discussions. Half the time I feel like resigning, but I certainly will be interested in the ed system but the way I have been going I would vegetate even more if I don't have to go to these meetings. Like today, I didn't dress until after 7 for an 8 o'clock meeting. Actually didn't get out of bed until 12:30. I go to sleep thinking of all the things I would do the next day (and get up early), but even though I wake up at 8 or 9 I can't bring myself to get out of bed. I certainly want to straighten out this house so why am I not doing it?

"I think that this 'journal' is in three different notebooks, all of which don't amount to a can of beans. If anyone bothers to read this, it may be confusing."

December 5, 1995: "I continue to be very unhappy and rather weak. I want to complete the house so that I could really decide whether to sell. I feel so very lonely. I don't really feel close to my kids. I am not very happy with myself or anything I do. If I were rich maybe I could be more content. Everything is an effort for me, even taking a shower. I don't know if I am afraid to dye or I am afraid of dying. I know that I don't have the guts to commit suicide. I have no hope for the politics in this country, but I don't involve myself in doing anything. All I want to do is nothing. Just sit around doing nothing. All I do is be pessimistic about everything."

August 16, 2000: "Great happening! I now have a new great computer and I now do E Mail etc. I have a long way to go but I am very excited and am making slow progress. Also have a fabulous new car, an Acura with a navigator. Own it, love it. Fancy and drives like a dream.

"Kids very helpful during my two stays in hospital."

August 27, 2001: "Let me try again to keep this going. I need help, but won't go. Medication should help. I shall ask Kellman to give me ritalin. Why not? What do I have to lose? I have to get the energy to do things. I would just like to stay in bed. Even when I come downstairs I quickly fall asleep sitting on the couch."

November 19, 2001: "My attitude toward life's so different from what it had been. I could always make a decision immediately. Now I can't make any decisions."

November 16, 2002: "It seems to me that as I get older it is harder & harder to make a choice. More than making a choice I am disgusted about my wake, sleep habits. I stay in bed much too late and unless I have some important-compelling-reason to go out I stay hanging out in my pajamas. Even if I do go out I have a hard time showering (the cold has been bothering me). So I make shift. Boy do I have the making of a dirty old bag woman."

December 22, 2003: "Goody has a second litter area. The bow window in the kitchen. She overturned a flower pot filled with dirt and was using it for a bathroom. Cleaned it all up. I think Goody knew she did wrong. She has been trying to get on my good side ever since.

"Maybe it's a good sign that I cleaned it up. There have been days, months, (years?) that I wouldn't have bothered. Now if only I could get myself to get out of my pajamas and generally do more. I seem to be unable to leave the house unless I must."

Heather and the kids and I took a short trip; when we got back, my mother was in the hospital. She'd had a worrying episode of shortness of breath and been diagnosed with congestive heart failure.

When I got there she was sleeping. Her hands were folded on her abdomen in a posture that would have looked prayerful, except that within the heart-shaped space between her hands was a little winged horse from the gift shop.

She always had to have something in her hands. I wondered if anyone else knew this about her, this small odd fact, or if it's the kind of thing that only your children will ever notice about you.

When she woke, she was surprised and happy to see me.

My mother's happiness on seeing me was one of the few things I could count on in life. I remembered her picking me up from school one day when I was in fifth grade. She was in the car, which was the first car we owned that came with power windows and power locks. It was still a novelty for us to raise the windows and lock the car by pressing a button. As I walked toward the car that day, my mother, happy to see me, kept making the locks jump up and down as if they were gleeful, and at the same time as I thought it was a little childish, I also thought it was funny. I remember thinking how odd it was that I gave someone this much happiness just by existing.

A nurse came into the room, and my mother, who had evidently made friends with her, said, "This is my son Brian. Have you read his books? Maybe you read the one called *Going Home in the Evening?*"

Both the nurse and I cracked up at the idea that she might have read it.

"I haven't read that one yet," she said. "But I'm sure it's a very good book."

That night I dreamed I had two weeks to live. In the dream I was divided between dread of nothingness and a sort of cozy acceptance. I was curled up in a ball in bed and planning on staying in that position.

I had more than two weeks to live, but she didn't. She had exactly two weeks.

Andrea, the head nurse from the Free Spirits unit, called to say that my mother had suffered another episode of breathlessness, and that they'd calmed her down with Ativan. She was resting now. Andrea said it was too early to tell whether it was a temporary crisis or a "change of status."

My sister visited her that night and reported that she was sleeping, hard to rouse.

The morning after that, Andrea called to say that they were now prepared to say that my mother *had* undergone a change of status.

I wasn't fluent in the language of nursing-home euphemisms, so I didn't understand what this meant, but I went to visit her that evening. Melinda was already there. My mother was in a state that I'd never seen or heard about or read about. It didn't seem to be a state that could be defined as a coma—she wasn't that far under—but it was deeper and heavier than sleep.

I sat at her bedside and put my hand on hers. Without opening her eyes, she grimaced and pulled her hand away.

She'd been lying like this for two days, without anything to eat or drink. There wasn't much to do but sit with her.

We waited by the bed in shifts. My sister and me; my sister and her husband and kids; Heather and my sister and me; Heather and the kids and me; Heather and me; just my sister; just me.

Cece, the morning aide, the aide she loved ("Maybe we can be co-teachers"), stayed late one evening to say hello to us. I told her how much she meant to my mother.

"We had a connection from the first," Cece said. "She's a lot of fun." She smoothed my mother's hair. "You should talk to her. She can hear you. She might not seem like she can hear you, but she can."

I knew she was speaking from experience—she'd worked there a long time—but I didn't believe it. My mother didn't seem to be just below the surface of consciousness, waiting for our words. She seemed far below, with her attention directed elsewhere. She seemed to be concentrating on where she was going and not on where she'd been. She was tunneling in the other direction.

I hadn't known that dying could be such hard work.

Even though we doubted she could hear us, we talked to her anyway.

During the past year, because of her deafness and her dementia, I had taken to talking to her in a sort of bellowing baby talk. But during the week in which she lay unconscious, I spoke to her as I had years ago, with a normal vocabulary and in a normal voice. It was as if I thought that if the nurses were right and she could hear us, she'd be receiving our words in a region in which her true, full consciousness, untouched by her dementia, still survived.

After "I love you," I didn't know what to say, but eventually other words came to me. I talked to her about all that she'd been and all that she'd given—what a good mother she'd been, what a good grandmother, what a good teacher, what a good activist. I told her how much I admired her for having seized control of her life when she was so young and for continuing, in so many ways, to live on her own terms. I told her about the folder of letters from parents I'd found, all of them thanking her for everything she'd done for their children. I reminded her how respected she was in her town and how beloved she was.

After that, I talked about everything she'd given me.

Not everything. A child can't possibly understand everything a parent has given. Rather, I talked about some of the things I appreciated most, and I discovered other things she'd given only as I talked to her.

I told her that when I was young, she had always made me feel safe. I'd always understood that she was a mother who'd do anything for us. We've all heard stories about mothers who'd somehow performed feats of strength like lifting up a car to free their trapped children. When I was growing up, I'd never had any doubt that if she needed to save us, she could have lifted a tank.

I told her she'd done more than anyone else to encourage me to be a writer.

When I was in high school, in the car together one afternoon, we were talking about my future, and I said I thought I'd like to be a psychologist.

"That's fine," she said. "That's a good thing to do with your life. But it's not the only thing you could be. You could be more than just that. You could be a writer."

She'd come from a family of artists, so she knew what the artist's life entailed. Her father and her brother had been artists, both of them kept aloft through their own belief in themselves rather than through anyone else's recognition.

Apart from his work in the theater, her father had been a painter and a sculptor. Most of his visual art was devoted to rendering the world he'd known when he was growing up in Lodz, Poland, all traces of which had been destroyed except for the images that remained in people's memories. There was a huge painting that still hung in her living room, of a wedding procession in Lodz, with about fifty different figures. When I was growing up, it was my favorite painting, because there were two little boys in it, one of them a member of the wedding group, dressed up stiffly in a suit and short pants, the other a street urchin, sticking his tongue out at the softer boy. Most people who looked at the painting probably didn't even notice them. Probably you took note of them only if you yourself were a little boy.

My uncle had been a composer of contemporary classical music, music that went beyond dissonance to realms even more obscure and unlistenable. "I hear harmonies no one else has ever heard," he once told me.

The two generations that preceded me believed being an artist is a worthy vocation, and that the seriousness of your devotion to it can't be measured by your income or your fame. My grandfather and my uncle, and my mother's feelings about them, opened the door to my life.

My father never stood in the way. Apart from one mild suggestion on the eve of my graduation from college—"You want to be a writer? You should go to journalism school"—he'd never tried to tell me what to do. At dinner with the two of them when I was twenty-four or twenty-five, after it had become clear that I was going to try to dedicate myself to writing fiction, he told me that I should be prepared for a tough road, one that would be especially tough in the first few years, when friends of mine who were on preestablished tracks—medical school, law school—would be making progress in a measurable way while my own progress would be much harder to gauge, and might seem, to an observer, to be nonexistent.

I'm not sure who is writing this now. The man who is older than my father was when he gave that advice, or the young man sitting in that restaurant listening to the advice and feeling touched that his father had thought about all this, and had thought about it sympathetically.

But it was my mother who encouraged me steadily. Because her father and brother had been artists, encouraging me came naturally to her.

This, at least, is what I'd always thought. It was only when I was sitting at her bedside, talking to her, although she was far below the surface, tunneling away, that I realized that I was failing to give her enough credit. Her father's way of being an artist had been wrapped up with a life spent constantly in flight from the family. And her brother's way of being an artist had meant writing music for large orchestras but rarely finding large orchestras to play it. It had been a life of steady frustration. Encouraging me to attempt to become any kind of artist hadn't been merely natural at all. It would have been just as natural if she'd begged me not to.

Sitting at her bedside, I reminded her, and I reminded myself, that she'd not only encouraged me, she'd helped me find my way. After I'd dropped out of college and glumly begun to form an adolescent conviction that there was no college anywhere that I wouldn't find stultifying, she saw an ad for a summer class that E. L. Doctorow was teaching at Sarah Lawrence, and, knowing that I loved *Ragtime* and *The Book of Daniel*, she'd suggested I apply. I did, and I loved working with him, and felt at home at Sarah Lawrence, and, again at her suggestion, I matriculated there. Twenty years after I graduated, I came back to teach there, and I've been there ever since. So that was another of the things she gave me, another of the things I thanked her for.

I'm not sure I became a teacher because of her, but the example of how to be a teacher that she'd set had guided me from my first day in the classroom.

She wasn't my only model. When I studied with Doctorow, he'd offer close critiques of what I'd written and then put my story aside and say, "But I might be wrong. And it really doesn't matter. The only thing that matters is that you keep writing. The only thing that matters is that you write your ass off." You got the sense that his teaching was animated by the belief that writers have to find their own direction, and that his task was just to accompany us a few steps along the way.

If his way of teaching felt immediately recognizable, immediately right, I think that was because it was so like my mother's way of teaching, her belief that the most important part of her job was helping her students start to learn to become independent-minded people. Years later, after I started to teach, whatever difficulties I had with the details—lesson plans, time management, thinking on my feet—I always knew what I was there for. The values I tried to bring to the classroom were the values I'd learned from her.

I talked to her about all this as I sat at her bedside on an evening when it was just the two of us. The recognition of how much I owed her was pouring through me. It was like the night in college when I took mushrooms and thought I saw the universe in a different way, except that in this case the effects turned out to be lasting.

I told her about all this in even more detail than I'm giving in these pages. It would be nice to think that she could hear.

On the fifth day—her fifth day without eating or drinking, her fifth day without opening her eyes—she began to breathe in a different way. She'd take in a great gulp of air and then lie unmoving for such a long time that you weren't sure she was going to breathe again. Then she would take in another gulp of air, and the cycle would repeat.

Later that day, Andrea told us that she was "actively dying." Which was another expression I'd never heard before.

If I had heard it before, I probably would have thought it sounded like a contradiction in terms. Dying, I would have thought, was something that happened to you, not something that you engaged in actively. But now I saw that it could be exactly that.

When we tried touching her hand, she would always pull it away. She gave no sign that she knew where she was or who we were, but she would withdraw her hand as if by touching her we caused her pain.

When my sister and I were with her that evening, an aide came to change her, and the two of us left the room. And then, miraculously, we heard my mother speaking again.

It wasn't what we might have hoped to hear. From the hallway we could hear her saying, "You bitch. Stop that. You bastard. You son of a bitch."

But it didn't matter what she was saying: it was a joy to hear her speaking again.

When the aide was finished and the two of us went back in, my mother still seemed exactly as she had when we'd left: deep down and far away. But since she'd just been speaking, we thought we'd finally be able to reach her, no matter how unreachable she seemed.

"I love you, Mom," my sister said.

Without opening her eyes, my mother responded: "Bullshit. Go to hell."

"I love you," I said.

"Well, I hate you."

She was to live another three days, but those were the last words anyone heard her speak.

I think a lot about her last words.

Maybe she believed she was still talking to the woman who'd been there a minute earlier, changing her diaper. Most of the women who worked there were Christians who felt moved by their piety to constantly tell her they loved her, and maybe she'd gotten into the habit of cursing them out whenever they did, and she was cursing Melinda and me as a reflex, without even knowing who we were.

But maybe it wasn't that at all.

She'd spent her life feeling as if the people she loved were depriving her. She'd spent her life thinking that happiness was within reach but was being withheld from her by the people she loved. She'd spent her life feeling as if she loved us more than any of us loved her.

Maybe she'd just had enough of it. And maybe, when she told me that she hated me, she knew exactly who she was talking to. Maybe this was the last and most important thing she wanted to tell me.

Sometimes I think I'd like this to be true. If she thought she was talking to an aide, then "Go to hell" and "I hate you" were just sad misunderstandings. How much better if she knew exactly who she was saying "I hate you" to.

I like the idea that she knew she was speaking to me, but I also like the idea that she wasn't speaking only to me—that she was using her last words to try to avenge every insult she'd ever suffered, from her father leaving, making her feel special and then running away, making her feel special and then running away, to her mother being cold to her as if she blamed her for her father's always running away, to her father saying she could never be an actor because she couldn't carry a tune, to both of her parents forbidding her from touching the piano because it was only for Heskel, to her husband not telling her when he was laid off and getting so angry when she found out that he didn't speak to her for weeks, to all the martinet principals who cared more about making sure she kept her classroom neat and the art projects put away at night and the fucking blinds evenly drawn than about the job she was doing with the children, to her daughter taking drugs all through high school and going out with men whose sole utility seemed to lie in how inconsiderate they were, how large a barrier they set up for her to conceal herself behind, to Dick's refusing to stop smoking or even to try, to his declaring they were never going out to dinner again after yet another fight in a restaurant about his smoking, despite his knowing that going out to dinner with him was one of the main pleasures of her life, it wasn't fair of him to say that, but he turned out to be right because he died just one week later, to the way she was treated by so many people in town as a lovable eccentric rather than a force to be reckoned with, did you not think I saw that, did you not think I saw the looks you exchanged at board of ed meetings when I got up to speak from the floor, I'd been a teacher in Teaneck for twenty years and then a board trustee for another twenty years and yet you ignorant pishers think you're entitled to roll your eyes when I get up to speak, don't mind her, she's past her prime, she's had her day, she's out to pasture, I know more about education than all of you combined, to the way Brian is so cold, to the way Melinda is so cold, the two of them so distant, Brian sometimes open and friendly but sometimes moodily withdrawing into coldness or even into rage just like his father, Melinda always available to talk to me but never willing to share anything of herself, Heather withholding the children from me, never letting me drive the children, for example, never letting me babysit, Brian says it's coming from him but I know it's coming from Heather, Heather so warm and lovely but keeping the kids from me and taking Brian away to California for two years, and Hal, the whatchamacallit, the superintendent of schools, who I had a crush on, who treated me as a joke, who flirted with me just for my votes, I knew he was manipulating me but I went along with it anyway, and Brian and Melinda taking my driver's license and keeping me trapped in that house, and that house that did everything it could to keep me trapped, spending years hating that house for trapping me, hating myself for letting it trap me, hating my children for not helping, hating my friends for not helping, hating everyone for withdrawing, but especially my children who could have made the difference, especially my children who could have taken me in, especially my children who could have thought about me, especially my children who could have taken me with them on vacations but never did, especially my children who could have asked me to stay over once in a while, especially my children who came over every night when I was no longer conscious, who stayed with me for long hours when I finally had no interest in talking to them anymore, who would never have treated me so well if I had come back to consciousness again, it would have been back to every two weeks hi Mom have some candy bye Mom, the two of them treating me well only when it was too late too late too late too late too fucking fucking fucking late. And even this, this monologue where you're trying to enter my thoughts, why won't you just let me be, instead you have to try to enter my thoughts and when you do you find nothing but grievance and deprivation, even here you get me wrong, because you miss so much of who I was. You're afraid to see so much of who I was. You started off writing this by saying that you wanted to find the parts of me that you left out of *The Dylanist*—that awful book, thank God nobody read it, thank God it was a bomb: my dignity, my love of education, my dedication to finding new ways to educate children, my devotion to helping children find the love of learning that's natural in all of us, my activism, I mean the fact that I was at meetings twice a week every week for my entire life, trying to make the world a little better, did you say anything about that? I don't think so, it was too much for you, and yeah, you mention it here, but only because you feel you have to, it's like obeying a fucking equal time law, but when you go back to writing about how you actually feel you go back to making a laughingstock of me again, taking in who I was is just too much for you, and speaking of too much for you, you haven't said a word about my marriage, because you're still trying to idealize it, and you're still trying to idealize your father, and I know he was a good man, I loved him too, I think he had as much integrity as anyone I've ever met, but did you ever stop to think about his remoteness, did you ever stop to think about what it was like to be married to that, you lived with us, did you ever see him hug me, did you ever see him give me a real kiss, instead touching my pinkie with his pinkie and saying, "A hearty handclasp," which he got from some movie, it wasn't even his original thought, did you ever see him put his arm around me in public, no you did not, there was something missing from him, God knows what those priests did to him, or *his* father, did you ever notice that he never talked about his father and if you asked him a question about his father he couldn't answer without stammering, and his stupid macho upbringing he could have worked on some of his problems maybe if not for his stupid macho upbringing, or whatever the Irish equivalent of macho is, he broke from his family and he broke from the Church and he became a communist but he never broke from his stupid macho upbringing, which meant that he couldn't work on his problems he could only pretend they didn't exist. I covered up for you for all those years, Dick, like those early years when you pretended you could drive, you never could drive, you could hardly drive five blocks without running up against the curb, but when we picked up Yeshua at the airport you bandaged your wrist to pretend there was something wrong with it that prevented you from driving, you looked like an idiot with your homemade sling. You were too bottled up to admit you couldn't drive, too bottled up to talk to me, when did you ever talk to me, that conversation in 1961 or whenever it was when you told me you didn't want to lose the kids, that was the only time you let your guard down with me in thirty-five years, that time and when your mother died and you cried two or three tears, boo hoo, did you even love her if so I never saw it, when we'd visit her you always wanted to get out of there even faster than I did, a peck on the cheek and then goodbye, that's how you treated her, did you ever take her seriously, what was she to you, and don't you think the kids saw that, don't you think Brian saw it and grew up thinking that's how a man should treat his mother, and then you died without telling me the story you were going to tell me, because you couldn't stop smoking, big strong man but you couldn't fight off a little fucking cigarette, so fuck you Dick, fuck you Melinda, fuck you Brian, fuck all of you. And Melinda you're the worst because you closed yourself off tight as a drum. When you had your bone marrow transplant and you were in the hospital you wouldn't fucking let me visit you. You wouldn't let your own mother visit you more than a few times a week. You said I got in the way, talking to your doctors too much, talking about myself too much to the doctors, but I'm your own mother, instead you had that friend whatshername come visit you all the time. How do you think that felt, to be stuck at home watching *Wheel of Fortune* while your daughter was in the hospital fighting for her life less than fifteen minutes away, but you couldn't be with her because she didn't want to see you? How do you think that felt? And Brian you're the worst because you made me a laughingstock in your book. Everybody else was bad to me once in the living but you were bad to me twice, in the living and in the writing down, thank God again it was a bomb. So fuck you. You could see how proud of you I was and you treated me like shit. You know you did. So go to hell. Go to hell is what I meant to say. It wasn't a mistake. I hate you is what I meant to say. You can think they were mistakes if that's what you want to think. You can think I meant to say those words to somebody else. You can think what you want. But what you can never do is change the fact that those were the last words I ever spoke to you. That was my triumph. That was my victory. That's what you can never take away.

Sitting at her bedside, I read a pamphlet a nurse had given us about the last stages of life. It described the kind of breathing she was doing—her halting, uneven inhalations—and said that in the next stage, the last stage, her breathing would change. The description of the way a person breathes in the last stage reminded me of the "death rattle" they always talked about in Russian novels and that had always seemed to me a myth, or maybe something that dying people used to do in the nineteenth century but don't do anymore. Apparently the death rattle was a real thing.

I kept waiting for the death rattle, but the death rattle didn't come.

On Wednesday evening, as my sister and I sat with her, her breathing began to change, but not in the way I'd read about. Instead of becoming more raspy and strained, it became more fluent. Suddenly she was breathing freely again. I thought she might be taking a turn for the better. I saw her regaining the health, such as it was, that she'd had before the week began. I saw us resuming the life of the past year—the Hershey's Kisses, the memories of the Children's Phone and my father's last night. The only difference, I vowed, was that I'd visit her more often.

This new way of breathing continued for twenty minutes. And then, just as suddenly as it had begun, it stopped. Her breathing returned to its former rhythm—one long breath, followed by a long frightening silence—but now it was even more labored, now it seemed even more painful.

She took another in the series of long breaths. We sat waiting in the silence for the next breath.

After two minutes or three minutes had passed, my sister said, "I think she's gone."

I'd seen death before. I'd seen family friends lying in open coffins. I'd seen my father, not yet embalmed, in the basement mortuary of a funeral parlor the day after he died. I remember that his hair was combed in a manner different from the manner in which he habitually combed it: someone else had combed his hair that morning. I remember that his ear had turned purple. I remember thinking that the force that keeps us alive serves to protect us in ways that someone like me can't even imagine, and that the moment that force withdraws, the savagery of the universe comes in and starts to devour us.

So I had seen death before. What I had never seen before was the passage from life to death.

It wasn't a sharp transition. It felt more like a movement along a continuum. A bit of moisture on her eyelid still glistened. The sweat on her neck, produced by the prodigious labor of the last few days, still gleamed. Her skin retained whatever quality it is that gives our living skin its aliveness.

I didn't want to leave the room too soon.

I had always wondered whether anyone can be sure about when consciousness exits the body.

We've all heard stories about people who were brought back to life after being pronounced dead—after two minutes, after five minutes, and even, in a few rare cases, after much longer than that.

So who can be sure that a flicker of consciousness doesn't remain even long past the point after which you can no longer be brought back?

As my sister and I sat with her body, I thought that if she'd really been able to hear us during the last few days, as all the aides had told us, it was conceivable that she could hear us still. My sister must have felt the same way. Both of us kept telling her that we loved her. And although we didn't talk about it, I think Melinda shared my reluctance to alert anyone in the nursing home. We wanted to delay as long as possible the moment when the bureaucratic machinery would go to work. So we sat there for a long time before I finally got up to tell the nurse.

Writing about it now, I wish we'd sat there longer. I'm not imagining that she could have been revived, and even if she could have been, I don't think there would have been any good reason to revive her. I'm only saying it's possible that even after half an hour, whatever it is that gives us consciousness was not entirely gone.

I wish we'd stayed with her for a day. That seems the proper length of time to stay with the body of someone you love. That seems like the proper amount of respect to pay to the woman who gave you life. If they find out someday that consciousness lingers in the body for a full day, in a form that's not measurable now but will be measurable in the future—well, that seems much more likely to me than the idea that consciousness dies out immediately.

We stayed until someone arrived from a nearby funeral home, zipped Tasha Morton into a bag, and took her away.

My dreams rarely rise to the occasion. Decades earlier, on the night my father died, I dreamed I'd lost my wallet. That was the whole dream.

When I thought about the dream in the days that followed, I found a way to make it seem less stupid than it had at first. Your wallet contains the proof of your identity. Concentrating on that idea, I was almost able to convince myself that the dream had been profound.

Now, the night my mother died, I dreamed I was giving a reading or a talk at a conference. There were only a few people in the room, and I was disappointed at the size of the audience. As I looked through my papers, preparing to speak, all of them got up and left.

Rather than feeling insulted, I felt liberated: I didn't have to give the talk at all.

In the morning I wondered what I could take from the dream. I imagined it was telling me that apart from everything else I was feeling, it was permissible to let myself feel a little bit of relief. I'd been set free of many taxing obligations.

But if this is what my unconscious was saying, then my unconscious was a bit of a dope. It was true about the obligations: I wouldn't be making midnight runs to Jersey to pick her up at the police station anymore. But it was a half-truth. One kind of work was over, but another was just beginning. We have our obligations to the dead.

When the novelist Henry James was dying, drifting in and out of lucidity, he received a visit from his beloved sister-in-law, Alice. Alice and her sons—his nephews—were the only family he had left.

When she asked if there was anything he wanted her to tell her sons, James said, in language that was probably more dramatic than he would have used if he hadn't been ailing and feverish and frightened about what awaited him, "Tell them to follow, to be faithful, to take me seriously."

When I first read this, years ago, I didn't think about it much. After she died, it came back to me, with a new meaning.

Tell them to take me seriously. Sometimes I think this was my mother's deepest wish.

We took their ashes, hers and his, to Rockport, Massachusetts, where we'd spent part of every summer when Melinda and I were kids.

I'd always hated the place. In the 1960s, you couldn't get decent TV reception there, and what made it even worse was that you could sometimes get *something*—but only a ghostly picture and scratchy sounds. What this meant was that I couldn't stop torturing myself, constantly adjusting the rabbit ears in the hope that if I could just find that perfect angle, I'd be able watch my shows.

Melinda, who was a bookworm, liked it there, but I was bereft without TV. Being able to watch TV would have meant being able to escape. I hated being cooped up with my family for two weeks at a time. The ocean was too cold and rough to swim in, and anyway I couldn't swim. The only thing we'd do during the day was sit on the scalding beach and read. I liked reading but I hated the beach.

The only activity I enjoyed there was our evening walk down Bearskin Neck, a narrow peninsula crowded with little stores. I liked the name "Bearskin Neck," I liked the idea of a peninsula (it's one of those ideas that appeal inexplicably to children, like "hot lava"), and I liked one of the stores, a general store with barrels of candy that you scooped out excitingly into plastic containers, which you then weighed on a shiny silver scale near the cash register.

Our parents had loved it there, so Melinda and I thought it was the right place to take them.

We liberated the bag of my father's ashes from the samovar, put it in a cardboard box beside the bag of my mother's ashes, and went to Rockport in early May. We took them to the tip of Bearskin Neck, where a rocky slope leads down to the ocean. The sun was high in the sky. The ocean was bluer than I'd remembered.

My sister was holding my mother's ashes and I was holding my father's. Heather and Mike and all four children were with us.

One of the earliest photos I have is of my sister and me in a spot very near the spot from which we were about to let the ashes of our parents loose in the wind.

If you can explain the nature of time to me, I'd be thankful.

I was wishing I were a believer. I was wishing I could believe that she'd already joined him, and that he was finally telling her the story he'd meant to tell her long ago.

We brought them to the edge of the water and waited until a moment when the wind from the ocean died down. My sister and I opened the bags and shook them. The ashes mixed a little in the air and scattered on the water.

When my father died, I was startled by how little he'd left behind. He had a few things in desk drawers but nothing that couldn't be cleaned out in a day. He'd made it weirdly easy for us.

My mother, of course, was different. There was the entire house to clean, and it took a month.

When it was finally cleaned and sold, I took one last visit to make sure we hadn't left anything behind. It was unrecognizable as the place my mother had lived in and besoiled for the past thirty years. Instead, it resembled the place it had been when they moved there. I'd forgotten what it looked like without the detritus of her despair filling every room.

So on that last day, the house was like a time machine.

I remembered how happy and hopeful she was when they moved there. She kept talking about "gracious living." My father thought taking on the responsibility of an old house at their age was a bad idea, but she'd loved the place so much that he'd gone along, grudgingly at first but then enthusiastically. And for a few years, living there had brought both of them pleasure.

I walked from one room to the other, calling out, "Mom? Dad?" and saying "I love you" and "I'm sorry."

I didn't quite know what I was sorry for. I was sorry they were gone. I was sorry their world was gone—most of the people they'd cared about, many of the places that had been their landmarks.

And I was sorry you can't stop time, because I knew that these few minutes of walking through the house would soon be over, and that I'd never set foot there again, and that even though I was walking through a house they'd departed, when I looked back on this afternoon it would seem in memory like the last afternoon I'd spent with them.

Well, Tasha, I guess this is it. This is my second try at writing about you, and I don't think there'll be a third.

I don't suppose this book adds up to a portrait of you that you would have enjoyed any more than you enjoyed the first one. But I did try to see you. I'm sure I got a lot of it wrong, but I tried to see you as you were.

No. I'd thought I was done, but that isn't the note I want to end on. I don't want to end with a passage about myself.

What should I end with, then? Not the woman leaping off the train. Not the woman arguing about religion with her nurse. Not even the woman sitting with her kindergartners and first graders on the floor of her classroom, helping them learn to read.

Instead, let me end with her voice on the phone after the first day of the conference on progressive education. Let me end with her saying that what she'd heard there had made her realize she still had some fighting to do. Let me end with her telling me—this was when she was seventy—that she knew she wasn't going to be able to fall asleep that night, because she was so excited about everything she was going to learn the next day.

Acknowledgments

For encouragement, support, criticism, etc., I wish to thank Paige Ackerson-Kiely, Robert Bedick, Jenny Doctorow, Emmett Donovan, Henry Dunow, Carolyn Ferrell, Lori Finsterwald, Todd Gitlin, Robert Gordon, Liselle Gottlieb, Amy Guay, Glen Gurner, Melinda Morton Illingworth, Rachel Kadish, David Kumin, Mark Levinson, Amelia Martin, Ilana Masad, Jo-Ann Mort, Gabriel Morton, Naomi Murphy, Robert Neumann, Fred Parnes, Howard Parnes, Amparo Rios, George Scialabba, Samantha Steiner, Ilja Wachs, and Lauren Wein.

About the Author

BRIAN MORTON is the author of five novels, including *Starting Out in the Evening* and *Florence Gordon*. He has been a recipient of the Guggenheim Fellowship, the Koret Jewish Book Award, and the Award in Literature from the American Academy of Arts and Letters, and a finalist for the PEN/Faulkner Award and the Kirkus Prize in Fiction. He teaches at Sarah Lawrence College and lives in New York.